As one of the world's longest established and best-known travel brands, Thomas Cook are the experts in travel.

For more than 135 years our guidebooks have unlocked the secrets of destinations around the world, sharing with travellers a wealth of experience and a passion for travel.

Rely on Thomas Cook as your travelling companion on your next trip and benefit from our unique heritage.

Thomas Cook **traveller** guides

IBIZA & FORMENTERA

Christopher & Melanie Rice

Thomas Cook

...ince 1873

Written by Christopher and Melanie Rice, updated by Nick Inman and Clara Villanueva
Original photography by Caroline Jones

Published by Thomas Cook Publishing
A division of Thomas Cook Tour Operations Limited
Company registration no. 3772199 England
The Thomas Cook Business Park, Unit 9, Coningsby Road,
Peterborough PE3 8SB, United Kingdom
Email: books@thomascook.com, Tel: + 44 (0) 1733 416477
www.thomascookpublishing.com

Produced by Cambridge Publishing Management Limited
Burr Elm Court, Main Street, Caldecote CB23 7NU
www.cambridgepm.co.uk

ISBN: 978-1-84848-392-7

Series Editor: Karen Beaulah
Production/DTP: Steven Collins

Printed and bound in Spain by GraphyCems

Contents

Introduction

To the Phoenicians, Ibiza was an island blessed by the gods and they came here to bury their dead. Ibiza was prized by the Carthaginians, who extracted salt from the pans near today's international airport, and by the Romans, who found the soil of Formentera well suited to growing crops. For the Moors, too, Ibiza was a land of plenty; their agricultural innovations are still discernible today in the Ses Feixes marshes. The Catalans saw Ibiza as a forward base in the Mediterranean, ripe for economic exploitation.

But it was the Ibizan landscape, and a way of life that had changed little over the centuries, that captivated the Beat Generation writers William Burroughs and Jack Kerouac in the 1950s. Folk singer Bob Dylan arrived a decade later. In his wake came the hippies, who found a Garden of Eden unsullied by material values and bad karma. They explored the island in search of mystical secrets and banged their drums in homage to the setting sun at Benniràs.

Much has changed in the last 50 years. Mass tourism has left an indelible mark on Ibizan society. It has generated a great deal of wealth and the hippies have largely been replaced by fashion designers and DJs, but large tracts of coastline have been sacrificed to insensitive urban development. The image many have today, of eyesore hotels and apartment blocks, of hordes of tourists packing the beaches and bars, is not an unfounded one. But neither is it wholly fair or accurate.

There is a lot more to Ibiza than this. Four different areas on the island have been declared a World Heritage Site thanks to its endemic seagrass, known as posidonia, its Phoenician sites of Sa Caleta and Puig des Molins, and the fortification of Dalt Vila. The latter, in Eivissa, the capital, is the walled city founded more than two and a half millennia ago. Sant Antoni is where the young come to party, dancing the night – or sometimes the day – away and also offers the wonderful bay which boasts three Blue Flag beaches. Sedate Santa Eulària is for those who want to give the hectic clubbing scene a wide berth. Visitors are charmed by the stark simplicity of its fortified church, built in the 16th century to ward off pirate attacks.

Not all of Ibiza's coastline is developed. With more than 50 beaches, there is still plenty of scope for discovering a remote cove. During the last decade, whole swathes of the two islands have acquired protected status.

The largest national park is Ses Salines, 810ha (2,000 acres) of wetland and coastal waters between Ibiza and Formentera. Within its confines are numerous hiking and cycling trails and untold opportunities for birdwatching – more than 200 species have been recorded to date. Visitors looking for solitude may find it in the pine-forested hills of Els Amunts and Sant Josep or on the terraced slopes of the Corona plain.

Ibiza is sometimes referred to as the 'white island': the hillsides are peppered with *casaments*, lime-washed cottages with metre-thick walls and tiny windows to regulate inside temperature. They are modelled on an Arab design over a thousand years old and never bettered, as the revolutionary modern architect Le Corbusier was quick to recognise. For genuine lovers of the island, this unspoilt 'other Ibiza' is the real one.

The land

Ibiza and Formentera form part of an archipelago that is situated southwest of Mallorca and about 170km (106 miles) east of the Spanish mainland. From the time of the ancient Greeks, they have been known as the Pitiusas or 'pine islands'. There are more than 50 in all, though most are uninhabited. Ibiza, the largest island in the group, has an area of 572sq km (221sq miles). Formentera is only 14km (9 miles) long from west to east, with a total area of 82sq km (32sq miles).

Landscape

There are two uplands in Ibiza, clearly visible as your aeroplane flies overhead. The Serra de Els Amunts range stretches all the way from Cala Sant Vicent on the northeast coast to Cala Salada in the west. Ibiza's highest peak, Sa Talaiassa (476m/1,562ft), rises not here but among the pine-covered hills of the Serra de Sant Josep in the southwest. The best farming land, characterised by a reddish clay soil, lies in the depression between the two ranges.

The rugged coastline to the west of Els Amunts, roughly from Cap Nonó to Cap d'Aubarca, is wild and inaccessible in places and consequently free of tourist development. By contrast, the sandy coves and beaches in the south and east have been heavily promoted, turning the ancient settlements of Santa Eulària and Eivissa into major holiday destinations. The wetlands in the southeast corner are of great ecological importance and form part of the protected Ses Salines National Park.

The topography of Formentera is relatively straightforward. Two plateaus, one to the south (Barbària), the other at La Mola in the east, are joined by a narrow isthmus with dunes and white sand beaches on either side. The salt lagoons of Estany Pudent and Estany de Peix are included in the Ses Salines National Park. Other features include a number of offshore islands and Es Trucadors, a finger-like promontory with more stunning beaches backed by dunes and pine woods.

Climate

Ibiza and Formentera have a Mediterranean climate with long, hot summers – warmer than Mallorca – and mild winters. Temperatures range from a daytime average of 15°C (59°F) between November and April, to 29°C (84°F) in August. Sunshine levels are also high, with a daily average of 10 or 11 hours from May to September, and rarely fewer than 5 hours in November and December. Cooling afternoon breezes tend to mitigate the high summer temperatures, which only really cause discomfort when the hot, dry wind known as the *leveche* blows in from Africa. Rainfall is moderate, the wettest months being March (51mm/2 inches) and October (77mm/3 inches). Virtually no rain falls in July. There is relatively little fluctuation in sea temperatures, which range from a high of 25°C (77°F) in August down to 13°C (55°F) in February.

Flora and fauna

Ibiza's southern latitude determines its flora and fauna. The ubiquitous pines, sabines and wild olive trees flourish on the upper hillsides, while on the lower slopes are junipers and rock roses. The rich soils of the central plains and valleys are ideally suited to the growing of olives, figs, vines, carobs (the fruit of the algarroba tree) and a variety of citrus fruits. Almonds are a speciality of the Santa Agnès plain, where blossom falls in January and February to create a snowscape effect. Bougainvillea, oleander and hibiscus all come into flower from July to September, adding more than a splash of colour, while cacti, agaves and palms thrive all year round. Rosemary, thyme and wild fennel are among the herbs used to season traditional Ibizan dishes. Numerous native plants are protected by environmental legislation, for example rock samphire (*Crithmum maritimum*), which grows on Es Vedrà. The soil on Formentera is not as productive because of the erosion caused by winds sweeping across the countryside during winter. Even here, though, vines, carobs and figs grow around El Mola and along the central isthmus, while clumps of rosemary and thyme can be found even in the wildest

Livestock is an important feature in the Ibizan landscape

Beautiful turquoise seas abound

reaches of the Barbària peninsula. The Ses Salines salt marshes near Eivissa and the salt lagoons of Formentera form an ecosystem unique to the Pitiusas. Here and around the coastline to the south of Sant Antoni is a vast 'prairie' of oceanic posidonia. This endemic Mediterranean plant, with roots, stalk, leaves and fruit, lives underwater to a depth of 40m (131ft). Posidonia contributes to coastal stability, protects beaches and is the habitat of numerous plant and animal species, some of which are threatened with extinction.

The Ses Salines National Park is also a bird sanctuary. The salt pans are one of the first ports of call for storks, herons and flamingoes and other migrant species on their way to Africa, while permanent residents include black-necked grebes, warblers and ospreys. Thekla lark, blue rock thrush and crag martin can be found around the cliffs, while the outlying islands support colonies of gulls and cormorants. Sightings of the rare Eleanora's falcon, an endemic Balearic species, are not uncommon on Es Vedrà.

Ibiza's marine life is equally varied. The island's fishermen bring in regular trawls of tuna, amberjack, barracuda, scorpion fish, spiny lobster, grouper and John Dory, while further out to sea one can expect to find turtles, hammerhead sharks and dolphins. Mention should also be made of the indigenous wall lizard *Podarchis pityusensis.* This hardy reptile, bright green and up to 7cm (3 inches) long, is easily spotted. Its natural habitat is barren, rocky land, but it can also be found near houses.

The environment

No one can pretend that the environment has not changed drastically in the Pitiusas over the last

50 years. Many people alive today can remember the thick mantle of pine forest around Cala Llenya or the beach at Cala Vedella when there wasn't a building in sight.

It was the Committee for the Defence of Ses Salines, formed in 1977, which drew the line in the sand against untrammelled urban development. This initiative spawned a variety of environmental pressure groups, from GEN (Grup de Estudi de sa Naturalesa) to Friends of the Earth, which have been campaigning ever since. The aim was not just to stop the property developers, but to promote understanding of the ecology by encouraging islanders to restore disused *fincas* (farms), wells and drystone walls and to adopt traditional, environmentally friendly agricultural methods. One successful campaign saved Cala d'Hort, which is one of the most valuable ecosystems in the Mediterranean (*see pp107, 110*). But this is a drop in the ocean. In 2006, a Greenpeace report warned that uncontrolled construction was causing widespread degradation of the environment of the islands. Other campaigns have focused on the Ses Feixes marshes (*see p58*), against the doubling of the width of the road from Eivissa to Sant Antoni and the island's expanding airport.

An artesian well at Ses Salines

History

c.4500 BC	Earliest evidence of human settlement on the islands. Cave dwellers, originally from the Iberian peninsula.
c.1600 BC	Renewed Bronze Age settlement on Ibiza and Formentera.
c.800 BC	Evidence that the Talayotic peoples of Mallorca and Menorca are trading with Ibizan settlers.
c.700 BC	The Ancient Greeks explore the Ibizan coastline but never settle. They call the islands the *Pitiusas* on account of the proliferation of pine trees.
654 BC	The Carthaginians capture and colonise the islands. They name the island Ibosim, after the god Bes. The capital becomes one of the most important ports in the Mediterranean. Trade and commerce flourish.
1st century BC	Following an earlier source, the geographer Diodorus Siculus writes (correctly) that Ibiza is about the same size as the Greek island of Corfu.
146 BC	Carthage is destroyed by the Romans.
123 BC	Roman conquest of the Balearic Islands. Ibosim is renamed Ebosus but not made part of the Roman Empire and instead granted Confederate status. Coins are minted with the Emperor's image on one side and the figure of the Carthaginian god Bes on the other. Commerce expands with the export of salt and lead.
AD 70	The Roman Emperor Vespasian demotes Ebosus to a mere municipality within the Empire.
421–5	The Vandals attack Ibiza and Formentera.
535	The Byzantine general Belisarius conquers the islands, which are incorporated into the eastern Empire.
693	Following the capture of Carthage by the Arabs, the islands are increasingly vulnerable to Moorish attack.

712 Ibiza and Formentera are incorporated into Visigothic Spain.

859 The islands are devastated by the Normans.

901–2 Ibiza and Formentera are conquered by the armies of the Emir of Córdoba and Islamicised, Ibiza being renamed Yebisah. The conquerors revolutionise agriculture, building irrigation ditches and planting rice, cotton and other crops. Olives and oranges are grown on hillside terraces, which still exist today.

1114 The combined fleets of Pisa and Aragón descend on Ibiza with the blessing of the pope. Declaring a crusade, they take the citadel, lay the city waste and massacre the Muslim population, but the islands remain under Arab control.

1235 On 12 August Catalan troops conquer Yebisah. Formentera is annexed in 1236. The islands are returned to Christianity, Catalan becomes the official language and the islanders are granted the right of self-government.

1261 A royal statute entitles the people of Ibiza to benefit directly from the profits of the salt industry.

1286 Ibiza and Formentera are formally annexed by the independent kingdom of Mallorca.

1299 A decree issued by Jaume II of Mallorca creates the *Universitat*, which becomes the municipal government of the islands. Ibiza is divided into four *quartons*: Santa Eulària, Sant Miquel de Balansat, Sant Antoni de Portmany and Sant Jordi.

1348 The Black Death reduces the population of Ibiza to around 2,000. By 1400 Formentera is completely uninhabited.

1359 An attack on Ibiza by Don Pedro 'el Cruel' is repulsed by Guillermo de Llagostera. Pedro el Ceremonioso subsequently repairs the walls of Dalt Vila.

1498 The Franciscans administer the new church of Nuestra Señora de Jesús, founded in the village of the same name.

1518	Spanish troops are billeted in Ibiza during Carlos I's offensive against Algeria. They sack the island after the government fails to pay them.
1554–5	Felipe II of Spain commissions the Roman military engineer Giovanni Battista Calvi to reconstruct the walls of Dalt Vila.
1584	Completion of the Ses Taules gateway sets the seal on the new Dalt Vila fortifications.
1587	The Dominicans receive permission to build a monastery within the walls of Dalt Vila.
1686	The Jesuits establish their first community on the islands.
1697	The repopulation of Formentera gets under way.
1708	The Dominicans found a free school in their monastery in Dalt Vila.
1767	The Jesuits are expelled from the islands.
1789	The Spanish monarchy commissions wholesale reforms on the islands. Public works programmes and modest improvements in health and education follow.
1800–15	Additional taxes, and the cost of the corsairs' allowances during the Napoleonic Wars and the Spanish War of Independence, impose severe hardship on the people of the islands.
1846	A new periodical, *The Ibizan*, is produced on the island's first printing press.
1848	Eivissa begins to expand beyond Sa Marina with the founding of the *Poble Nou* (New Town).
1871	The Spanish government sells the salt pans of Ses Salines to a private company.
1875–1900	Emigration to the United States, Cuba and South America intensifies, as many Ibizans, especially young males, find it impossible to make a living on the island.
1885–1912	Construction of the new port in Eivissa harbour

	entails closing the straits between the islets of Grossa, Plana and Botafoc.
1892	Ibiza gets its own daily newspaper, the *Diario de Ibiza*.
1936–9	The Spanish Civil War. Ibiza falls to the Nationalists and is placed under the authority of a military governor, General Goded. People divide along Nationalist and Republican lines and there are massacres on both sides, as well as wholesale destruction of property. Franco's forces imprison Republicans in Dalt Vila and establish a concentration camp in La Savina, Formentera.
1950	The Balearic Islands receive 98,000 visitors annually.
1958	Ibiza Airport opens to commercial traffic.
1960	During the following decade Ibiza is colonised by hippies.
1970	The Balearic Islands now welcome around 400,000 visitors annually.
1975	Death of General Franco, ending more than 35 years of autocratic government and the suppression of the Catalan culture.
1983	Catalan becomes an official language on a par with Castilian Spanish.
1986	Spain joins the EEC (later the EU).
1999	Parts of Ibiza, including Dalt Vila, are declared UNESCO World Heritage Sites. A progressive regional coalition comes to power and introduces the controversial ecotax.
2003	The Conservatives are returned to power in regional elections and the ecotax is abandoned. About 85 per cent of the population of the Balearics earns a living from tourism.
2004	Socialist leader José Luis Rodríguez Zapatero becomes president of Spain.
2008	Ibiza island council orders the end to day-time clubbing after 6am, the so-called 'after hours' opening.
2011	Local elections due on Ibiza and Formentera.

Politics

Issues of national and international significance are as much debated in Ibiza and Formentera as anywhere but local politics are mainly dominated by a perennial debate over the pace and direction of development of the islands: how far economic development led by tourism should be encouraged and how far it can or should be balanced with the need to maintain the islands' identity and sense of community, and protect their remaining natural spaces.

Autonomy

As the cornerstone of Spain's transition from dictatorship to democracy, a new constitution was passed in 1978 recognising the varying natures and needs of the different parts of the country. This constitution established the principle of a division of powers between three tiers of government – state, region and local – which have appropriate tax-raising, legislative and executive powers.

Many of the functions of the state are devolved to the *comunidades autónomas* or autonomous regions. Along with the larger islands of Mallorca and Menorca, Ibiza and Formentera form part of the Balearic Islands under the Govern de las Iles Balears with its own prime minister (since 2007 Presidente Francesc Antich, backed by the Socialist parliamentary group), democratically elected parliament and ministries based in the capital of the Balearics, Palma de Mallorca.

Beneath this regional government, Ibiza and Formentera each has a *consell insular*, a mini-island government consisting of a *presidente* (council leader), a *pleno* (assembly) and departments which provide the various services. Since the elections of 2007, Ibiza has been governed by the Grupo Progresista, a coalition of the Socialist Party and a relatively new party (formed in 2006) called Eivissa pel Canvi (which means Ibiza for Change). The leader of the council is Xico Tarrés Marí. The opposition is formed by the right of centre Partido Popular. New elections, in which foreign residents can vote, will be held during 2011.

The island of Ibiza is subdivided into five municipal areas: Eivissa (the capital), Sant Antoni de Portmany (west), Sant Joan de Labritja (north), Sant Josep de sa Talaia (south) and Santa Eulària des Riu (east). These municipal areas are further broken down into parishes.

Hot topics

The perennial issue of local politics is how far – and how fast – development should go on a small island in which space is finite. That is, how to balance the protection of the traditional *ibizenco* way of life and its heritage (both man-made and natural) with the need to ensure long-term stable economic activity to create prosperity and employment.

While some people see the island's investment in mass tourism since the 1960s as a great success, others think that it has been at the cost of the island's identity. Such critics believe the priority should be given to attracting 'quality' tourism: that young, single partiers should be replaced by more discerning couples and families.

The arguments are compounded by accusations of corruption, caciquism and profiteering: that decision makers in the past have arranged things for the benefit of their own pockets and their cronies. Often the clincher to any debate is employment: which course of action creates more jobs for locals.

A pristine cove in the Cala d'Hort Nature Reserve

The Catalan connection

On 8 August 1235 the forces of Jaume I of Aragón and Catalunya, under the command of Guillem de Montgrí, archbishop of Tarragona, captured the citadel of Yebisah after a short siege, so ending more than four centuries of Arab rule. Tradition has it that the invaders entered through a secret tunnel following a tip-off from the governor's brother – the pair had fallen out over a woman. Whatever the truth, the Catalan invasion changed the course of Mediterranean history.

Golden age

The crown of Aragón imposed its own laws and institutions, insisted on the use of the Catalan language and restored the Catholic religion. But the conquerors were generous in victory.

Local and Catalan flags fly on Ibizan public buildings

By the *Carta de Franquicias* the islanders gained a measure of self-government, an independent judiciary, tax exemptions and the abolition of conscription. They were also allowed to exploit the highly lucrative salt industry. The Pitiusas were now under the protection of a powerful mercantile state with possessions scattered throughout the Mediterranean. The population increased as settlers from the mainland were encouraged to colonise the islands. The capital – renamed Eivissa – prospered and was given its own administration, the *Universitat*, but at the expense of the countryside, which rapidly became impoverished. Ibiza was already in decline when the Spanish abolished the Catalan administration following the War of the Spanish Succession (1702–14).

Revival

At the time of Franco's death in 1975, the survival of Catalan culture was in the balance. For the previous 40 years, the Fascist regime had suppressed every expression of regionalism in Spain. The Catalan language was confined to the home. Newspaper, radio and TV output was exclusively in Castilian (Spanish), and Catalan was

Eivissa, Jaume I of Aragón's capital

outlawed in offices and schools. In 1983, the new regional government set about reversing the trend, but it was no easy task. Ironically, the decade following the end of Franco's rule saw the proportion of Catalan speakers fall. The tourist boom of the 1960s had fuelled a population increase of more than 40 per cent as migrants from the poorer regions of southern Spain and North Africa came looking for work. Fear that Catalan culture might be swamped by outsiders has led to a vigorous, at times aggressive, promotion of the language. This in turn has led to resentment and some outright opposition. At the local level, a group consisting of mainly wealthy residents from the mainland protesting against the introduction of Catalan street names in the small community of Jesús in Ibiza, succeeded in having the scheme overturned. Yet Catalan, though a minority language, is spoken by around ten million people, from Catalunya Valencia and the Balearic Islands to Sardinia and the Pyrenees – more in fact than speakers of Danish and Norwegian.

While many people in the Balearics sympathise with the Catalans' increasingly strenuous demands for Madrid to recognise their region's 'nation-status' (if not independent nationhood), few have any wish to see the islands exerting their separateness in a similar way.

Culture

Visitors who notice something familiar about the whitewashed, cuboid houses of the Ibizan countryside are not mistaken. Functional, and minimalist in form, the humble casament *influenced the development of two important schools of 20th-century architecture: the Bauhaus and the Modern Movement. Erwin Broner and Josep Lluís Sert, both disciples of Le Corbusier, did more than anyone to promote the* estilo ibicenco, *both internationally and on the island.*

Domestic architecture

The *casament* (described by Sert as 'the timeless root of a house both rational and full of sculptural force') is arguably the most enduring legacy of the Arabs to the peoples of the Pitiusas. A key component is the metre-thick double walls, the intervening space filled with rubble and mortar, which hardens like adobe. Designed to regulate the temperature, these walls are remarkably successful in retaining the heat in winter and holding it at bay during the long hot summers. The same logic dictates the number of openings – kept to a minimum, but strategically placed to let in the maximum amount of light. The roof is flat and waterproofed with charcoal, while precious rainwater is collected in tiled gutters on either side.

Inside, the rooms are arranged around a large central space, the *porxo*, where the extended family traditionally gathered at meal times or for weddings and other celebrations. The bedrooms, living quarters, stables and storerooms are all under the one roof. If more space is required, the modular form allows any number of identical units to be built on to the main structure.

Outside is the *porchada*, a canopied porch cool enough for the afternoon siesta or even for sleeping through the sultry nights of July and August. Other elements of the *casament* are the *pozo* (well), usually sited close to the porch, and a small garden for growing herbs and vegetables.

Where to see traditional houses

The best examples are in the Els Amunts Natural Park in the north of the island, especially around Sant Vicent de Sa Cala. Otherwise, visit the Ethnographic Museum in Santa Eulària, which is actually located in a *casament*. There are numerous instances of modern houses influenced by the traditional Ibizan style; for example, the house at Carrer de Sa Bomba 18 in Sa Penya, Eivissa, is the work of Le Corbusier, no less.

Festeig

The traditional courting ritual (*festeig*) was observed until comparatively recent times and took place in the *porchada*. A girl of marriageable age would leave the house, dressed in her finest clothes and chaperoned by her father, to meet prospective suitors. Like the princes in a fairy tale, each would approach her in a predetermined order and do his best to win her over. This was a leisurely ritual that might continue over several consecutive afternoons. The community would know that the girl had made up her mind when she appeared at Mass, wearing a ring on every finger but not the thumb.

Music and dance

The traditional ceremonial dance, the *ball-pagès*, is rooted in courtship ritual, though its origins are more primitive. Anthropologists have noted pronounced similarities with a war dance introduced to Russia from Kurdistan by the Cossacks. The protagonists of the Ibizan folk dance, male and female, each have an assigned role. The woman, though far from passive, is always submissive, never looking her partner directly in the eye. The male, on the other hand, struts about like a cockerel – the symbolism is deliberate – eschewing specific steps in favour of wild leaps and bounds.

Colourful folk display in Eivissa's town hall

Castanyoles (castanets) are larger and louder than their Spanish cousins

Following a signal on the castanets, the dance begins at a slow tempo with the *curta* (literally, 'short'). The female waits on her partner, who approaches in a swaggering, extrovert manner. She responds by tracing figures of eight on the ground, moving her body in time with the music. The tempo now accelerates, heralding the second part of the dance, known as the *llarga* (long). Provoked by the woman's modesty, the male is emboldened, his body language suggesting more than a touch of arrogance. The female makes ever-widening circles around him until, driven to the point of distraction, he reaches her with a single spectacular jump, only to crown her with his hands before kneeling submissively at her feet.

The musical accompaniment is provided by a small ensemble of folk instruments: the *castanyoles* (castanets), which are larger (and louder) than the Spanish equivalent; a single flute, traditionally made from oleander and encrusted with metal; the *reclam de xeremies*, a double reed instrument belonging to the clarinet family, and the *tambor*, a decorated drum made from pine wood.

Where to see traditional folk dancing
Folk troupes perform at the annual patronal festivals of all major villages in Ibiza and Formentera. In addition, the folk-dance groups *Colla de Vila* and *Colla de Sa Bodega* perform every Friday throughout the summer in the Es Baluard de Sant Pere, Eivissa, starting at 9.30pm in July & Aug and at 9pm in Sept.

Costume

The elegance of the *traje blanco*, the traditional folk dress worn by women in summer, inspired the Ad Lib fashion designers of the 1970s.

The essential element is a white blouse and flounced, multilayered skirt, invented, so it is said, to convince marauding pirates that the wearer was pregnant. In winter, traditionally Ibizan women change into the *gonella*, a pleated, black woollen tunic with buttoned sleeves, worn under a delicately embroidered bodice. A linen shawl is drawn over the shoulders and fastened at the chest, while fibre espadrilles and a broad-brimmed hat, decorated with flowers, complete the ensemble. The most important ornament is the *emprendada*, a tiered necklace of silver, gold and coral, with an elaborate jewelled cross at the centre. The male costume is more straightforward: white linen shirt with ruffled, stand-up collar, white trousers, red sash, black waistcoat and red, tasselled beret.

CATALAN LANGUAGE

A Romance language with roots in medieval Latin and Provençal French, Catalan was fully formed by the end of the 11th century, the first written texts appearing shortly afterwards. In Ibiza and Formentera the dialect is known as *Eivissenc*. This preserves some of the Balearic vocabulary already outmoded in Catalunya itself, most obviously the old definite articles *es*, *sa* and *ses* for *el*, *la* and *les*, which are commonly used in place names. *Eivissenc* also incorporates some words from the Valencian dialect of Catalan as well as some indigenous words, such as *major* instead of *avi* (grandad).

The Ethnographic Museum in Santa Eulària

Festivals and events

Three annual celebrations – the pre-Lenten Carnaval, Easter and Corpus Christi – vary in date as they are centuries-old religious festivals. Carnaval (see below) *also depends on the fall of Lent. Corpus Christi falls seven weeks after Easter.*

Each community in Ibiza and Formentera has its *dia patronal* or patron saint's day. On these colourful occasions everyone lets their hair down and villagers wear the traditional folk costume, including the *emprendada*, a necklace handed down from mother to daughter (*see p21*).

Village saints' days include:
12 February – Santa Eulària
19 March – Sant Josep
5 April – Sant Vicent
25 July – Sant Jaume (Formentera)
4 November – Sant Carles
16 November – Santa Gertrudis

January

Cap d'Any *1 January.* In the capital, New Year celebrations centre on Plaça Vara del Rey. Revellers swallow 12 grapes, one for each stroke of midnight.
Cabalgata de Reyes *5 January, Eivissa and other main towns.* Procession of the Three Kings on the eve of the day when Spanish children traditionally receive their Christmas presents.
Festa Patronal de Sant Antoni de Portmany *16–17 January.* Blessing of pets and other animals on Passeig des Fonts. Local delicacies, including sausages, are grilled on bonfires.

March–April

Carnaval Fancy-dress parades and mischief, including the gentle ribbing of local public figures.
Semana Santa *Week before Easter.* On the last three days of Holy Week images of Jesus and the Virgin are carried through the streets in solemn procession. The most impressive events take place in Eivissa and Santa Eulària on Good Friday.
Feria Náutica *Mid-April, Santa Eulària.* Boat fair in the marina.

May

Anar a Maig *First Sunday of the month, Santa Eulària.* Procession of horse-drawn carts bedecked with flowers. Firework display and folklore festival, plus local agricultural and motor fairs.

Eivissa Medieval *Second weekend of the month (see pp24–5).*
Moda Ad Lib *End of the month, Eivissa.* Fashion parades attract Spanish TV celebrities and show-business people.

June

Corpus Christi *Eivissa.* The host is carried in procession from the Cathedral to the church of St Elm, honouring a 14th-century tradition.
Focs de la Nit de Sant Joan *23–24 June.* Huge bonfires are lit to mark St John's Eve, the shortest night of the year. In Eivissa, celebrations focus on Plaça Enrique Fajarnes.

July

Dia de la Verge de Carmen *16 July, coastal towns and villages, especially Eivissa, Sant Antoni and Es Cubells (Ibiza) and La Savina (Formentera).* Feast day of the patroness of seafarers. Statues of the Virgin are carried to the harbour, where fishing boats, lit by Chinese lanterns and festooned with streamers and pennants, are blessed by a priest.

Semana Santa procession

August

Festa Patronal *First two weeks of August, Eivissa (see p25)*
Día de Sant Bartolomeu *24 August, Sant Antoni.* Firework display in the harbour with swimming races, slingshot competitions and folk concerts.
Sant Agusti. The married men of the village challenge the bachelors to a football match.
Jazz Festival *Last week of the month: Dalt Vila, Eivissa.* Concerts showcase young musical talent.

September

Festa Patronal de Sant Miquel de Balansat *29 September.* Village fair. Pigs are slaughtered and consumed as *butifarrò* (black pudding) and other delicacies.

October

Festa Pagesa *Sunday mid-October, Es Cubells and Sant Antony de Portmany.* Country dancing performed by troupes from around the island.

December

Festa Patronal de Sant Francesc, Formentera *3 December.* Bonfire outside the church, followed by a roast pork feast.
Nadal *6 December–5 January, Eivissa* Christmas fair on Plaça Vara del Rey.
24 December, across the islands Churches are decorated with flowers for candlelit midnight mass.

Dalt Vila festivals

Eivissa's medieval festival

On the second weekend in May, Dalt Vila springs to life with a major festival marking the World Heritage status conferred on the city by UNESCO in 1999. The first celebration took place the following year and now attracts an estimated 100,000 visitors. The aim is to celebrate Eivissa's rich architectural and cultural heritage – part of the proceeds goes to restoration and conservation projects within the walled town. In the days leading up to the festival, Dalt Vila's winding streets echo to the sound of hammer and nails as the stalls (more than 100 in all) are erected. Meanwhile, volunteers hang bunting, flags and pennants, and install flaming torches for the evening events.

The show gets under way with a welcome concert from the Musikkapelle Ciutat d'Eivissa (City of Eivissa Music Band). There are around two dozen shows and theatrical events each year, held in venues all over the town: from Ses Taules and Mercat Vell to the cathedral square and the cloisters of the Town Hall. The theme throughout is medieval and Renaissance, traditional and esoteric. Past events have included organ recitals, sephardic singing, Arab dancing displays, Commedia dell' Arte and tongue-in-cheek pageants like 'Eivissa against the Grand Turk' or 'Moors versus Christians'. To attract the children there are archery and falconry displays, not to mention donkey rides. When they're not being entertained, visitors can browse the stalls, manned by locals decked out in medieval costume. Traditional handicrafts are represented with embroidery, woodwork, ceramics and basket weaving. You can buy decorative candles and joss sticks, jade necklaces, Ibizan liqueurs, aromatic shampoos, medicinal herbs, honey, jam, wines and cheeses – you name it. At supper time spicy sausages are cooked over an open fire and served with bread rolls and a glass of wine or beer. With

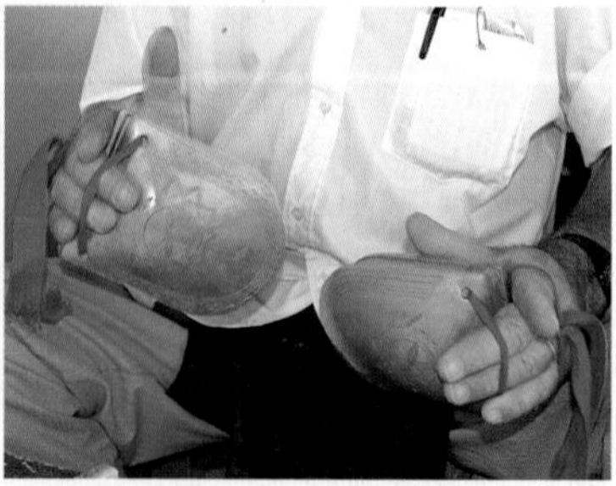

Playing *castanyoles*, Ibizan castanets

Colourful dancing displays are the hallmark of Ibizan festivals

incomparable views of the harbour from the battlements, what more could anyone wish for? Don't miss it.

Festa Patronal

Dalt Vila's other important summer festival, held from 1–8 August, honours the city's co-patrons, Our Lady of the Snows (Mare de Déu de les Neus, 5 August) and Sant Ciriac (8 August). The feast of St Ciriac also marks the day when, in 1235, the Arabs were expelled from the city by the Catalans, led by Guillem de Montgrí. In the morning there is a solemn high mass in the cathedral, followed by a procession to Sant Ciriac's chapel and a folk-dancing exhibition. In the evening everyone heads for Puig des Molins and the traditional *berenada* (supper) of *coca amb pebrera* (pastries with red peppers), buns and watermelons. The highlight is the watermelon fight in Es Soto beneath the city walls. Throughout the festival, the confraternities, called *collas*, put on shows of traditional village dances (*ball-pagès*) to the accompaniment of flutes, drums and castanets. The *Colla de la Vila* performs in front of the cathedral on the evening of 5 August, the *Colla de Sa Bodega* at the quayside on the following evening, traditionally the fishermen's day (there's a ceremony at the Monument to the Corsairs). All these festive acts are rounded off with stunning fireworks illuminating the city walls and the Mediterranean beyond.

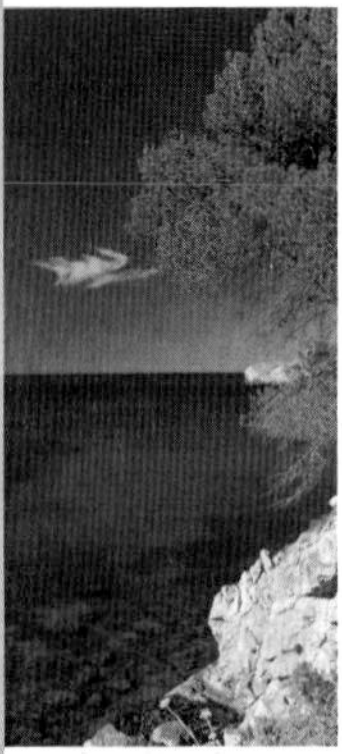

Impressions

With 300 days of sunshine a year and four hours a day even in January, Ibiza is an all-year holiday spot. The hottest period, from June to late September, is also the busiest, when hotel prices, car rental charges and club tickets peak and the population increases tenfold.

When to go

If you are holidaying in July and August, try to do your sightseeing in the mornings (the earlier the better) and then spend the afternoon lingering over lunch or taking a nap. Remember that shops and boutiques stay open until midnight, so you can buy gifts and souvenirs in the cool of the evening. Out of season, Ibiza is almost unrecognisable. The beaches are empty and the roads infinitely less crowded. Arrive early in the autumn and you will be able to take advantage of the end-of-season sales in the shops and boutiques. In spring the flowers are in bloom and the countryside, freshened by spring rains, is ravishing. Winters are mild with little rainfall, although sudden downpours and occasional storms can be expected. Swimming is possible from May to November and even beyond, although only the hardiest souls take the plunge in February. If you travel out of season, you will have more opportunity to meet the islanders and perhaps practise your Spanish and Catalan.

What to wear

Pack light, airy clothes for July and August as it is usually hot at night, too. Some form of head covering is essential to avoid overexposure to the sun.

In May, June and September it is a little cooler in the evenings, so a light jacket or jumper is a good idea. Bring a waterproof, as the odd shower is always a possibility. While the climate from October to April is mild, you may well need a jumper and a waterproof.

There are no dress codes, except in the most exclusive hotels, restaurants and clubs.

Information

The best tourist office is in Eivissa's port area (*see p188*); there is also an office at the airport. The offices in Santa Eulària (*www.santaeulalia.net*), Sant Antoni and the port of La Savina (Formentera) are equally obliging, but brochures and leaflets tend to be more localised. The website *www.illesbalears.es* has some general information on Ibiza and Formentera. All tourist offices supply lists of accommodation, bars and restaurants, town plans (including an excellent map of Dalt Vila), bus timetables, etc. They will also have information on organised excursions by train and hot air balloon, as well as walking trips and boat trips. Similar excursions are available on Formentera.

Going local

There are certain times of the year in Ibiza when you may hear yourself asking the question: 'Am I in Spain?' German and English seem more common than Catalan, and every other bar and restaurant offers fish and chips, Sunday roasts and Sky Sports. To enjoy the authentic Ibiza – Formentera presents less of a problem in this respect – spend more time inland or in the smaller coastal settlements. Pick up

Statue in Plaça des Parc, Eivissa

Take your pick from the stunning bays on Ibiza

a smattering of one of the local languages (Spanish or Catalan) – a little goes a long way and will earn you respect from locals. Try to adapt to the Spanish way of life: choose a restaurant that serves local or Spanish dishes, enjoy a leisurely lunch, then take a short snooze – a recent survey confirmed what the locals have always believed, that a daily 30-minute siesta is good for you.

On the beach

Most large beaches have Red Cross stations and lifeguards, and buoys mark the areas safest for swimming. Hidden rocks can be treacherous, especially in the smaller coves along the north coast. There are two official nudist beaches, at Es Cavallet (favoured by gay tourists) and Aigües Blanques. Topless bathing is acceptable almost anywhere. Beach umbrellas are available for hire in the resorts, but you will need to bring your own to the more isolated coves. The one essential item is a high-factor sunblock. Bring plenty, reapply after swimming ('water resistant' is a misleading term), and cover *all* exposed areas, including the tops and soles of feet. Avoid sunbathing between noon and 4pm, when the sun is at its hottest, and beware of dozing off on the sand or at the poolside. One dose of sunburn can ruin a holiday. Drink plenty of water to avoid dehydration. Beach restaurants and *chiringuitos* (snack shacks) are usually closed from the end of September to at least the beginning of May. One final word of warning: bring

The rocks of Es Vedrà and Es Vedranell rise from beautifully clear waters

only the cash you are likely to need, and never leave bags unattended – thieves never take a holiday.

Getting around

Eivissa airport is at Ses Salines, about 7km (4 miles) from the town. The taxi fare is reasonable, though you will save money by taking the bus (hourly service from early morning until 11.30pm in winter; until later in summer).

Buses: Connections between the main towns – Eivissa, Sant Antoni and Santa Eulària – are excellent, though at peak times buses are crowded and you may have to stand. There are regular services to Port de Sant Miquel and Portinatx on the north coast and to some popular beaches – Es Canar, Port des Torrent and Ses Salines, for example. Other destinations are less easily accessed, including all those on Formentera. For information see *www.ibizabus.com*

Boats: Vessels ply the coastline around the three main resorts and are a pleasant and leisurely way of getting about. Demand is high, so do not leave buying until the last minute. In season, there are regular shuttle services to nearby beaches (Ses Salines, Port des Torrent, Es Canar).

Ferries: The trip to Formentera only takes around 30 minutes, with ferries operating daily from 8.30am to 8pm from Eivissa's Estación Marítima (*www.directferries.es*).

Taxis: Taxis are white with a coloured diagonal stripe across the front door. A green light signals that the taxi is for hire. Taxis are relatively inexpensive. There are no meters – prices are fixed according to the destination. Rates are posted outside the main taxi ranks and are available from tourist offices – alternatively, consult the driver beforehand. The round-the-island excursion is useful for a quick orientation.

Cycling: This is by far the most enjoyable way of getting around and Formentera presents few problems as most of the terrain is relatively flat. There are numerous bike-hire firms on the quayside at La Savina – hire a mountain bike if you intend travelling to the far end of the island, which involves an uphill climb. Cycling on Ibiza involves steeper gradients and you'll need to be fit. There are only a few rental agencies – ask at the tourist office for details. Pick up a copy of *Rutes Cicloturisme*, which outlines itineraries of between 24km (15 miles) and 56km (35 miles), indicating gradients, to use in conjunction with a more detailed map. *See also www.ibiza.travel/en/cicloturismo.php*

Hiking: The series *Rutas des Falcó* (also available from the tourist office) sets out walks of varying levels of difficulty, all of which are signposted. As part of the 'Carreranys de Sant Josep' initiative, eight walks from 3km (1³/4 miles) to 15km (9 miles) around Sant Josep have been outlined; ask at the tourist office for the booklet. When out walking, wear comfortable shoes or boots with a good grip. Take a detailed map as insurance against getting lost. Break yourself in gently, allow plenty of time and never set out in bad weather. Bring food, plenty of water, and sunblock. Always ensure that you wear a head covering of some description and do not forget your binoculars!

Driving: Ibiza has a good, fairly comprehensive road network. Surfaces are in an excellent state of repair (better, in fact, than many on the mainland), but a four-wheel-drive vehicle may be necessary to negotiate the dirt tracks leading to the more remote coves and beaches. Lack of rain during the summer can mean slippery surfaces – a particular hazard for two-wheel-drive vehicles. There are petrol stations in main towns and settlements but fewer along the roadside, so fill the tank before setting out. Observe speed limits and remember that many coastal roads have challenging hairpin bends. The sign *Ceda el paso* at junctions and crossroads means 'give way to the right'. Avoid driving at night, as roads are poorly lit and some clubbers will inevitably be under the influence of drink or drugs (*see pp182–3*).

Bicycles resting at Platja Llevant, Es Trucadors peninsula, Formentera

Tourism and immigration

Ibiza and Formentera receive almost two million visitors a year, mainly from Britain (34 per cent) and the rest of Spain (30 per cent). Compare this with a figure of 98,000 for the entire Balearic region in 1950 and the scale of the influx becomes apparent. Tourism has had a profound impact, not least on the island's economy. Traditionally an agricultural society, today more than four out of five islanders depend on tourism, directly or indirectly, for their survival.

When the number of visitors fell by around 10 per cent in 2002, the first drop in more than a decade, alarm bells started to ring. Hoteliers, property developers, shopkeepers, politicians, as well as the man and woman in the street, pored over the statistics and began analysing possible reasons for the downturn. All kinds of suggestions were put forward: the terrorist attack on New York on 11 September 2001, cut-price holidays on the Turkish coast, the crisis in the German economy, and the ecotax.

In fact, things were not as black as they seemed. 'Quality' tourism, for example, remained largely unaffected, with the yachting industry reporting 'business as usual' and the increasingly important gay market equally untroubled. However, it is true

The sheltered beach at Figueretes, near Eivissa

that tourists, Germans especially, are spending considerably less than they were a decade ago. Resorts like Sant Antoni have become overdependent on package holidays and mass tourism (the sector hardest hit by the recession), with clients tending to opt for shorter stays. Ibiza continues to rely heavily on the youth market, a loyal constituency up to now, but a demanding one, constantly on the lookout for something new or different. The clubbing scene, one of the island's most important sources of tourist revenue, remains popular with Brits and now has a wider European following. Celebrity appearances by the likes of Kate Moss, Naomi Campbell and Cristiano Ronaldo have helped keep clubs Pacha, El Divino and the rest in the public eye. That said, the tourist industry will have to broaden its base – attracting families and Third Age visitors, and developing a winter season – something Mallorca has been doing successfully for years. In other words, Ibiza's image may well have to change.

The coffee tables of hotel lounges across the island are littered with glossy brochures offering a bewildering variety of properties for sale. Succumb to temptation and you will be joining the 15,000 foreign residents (mainly British and German) who have already set up home here. This represents a

Ibiza is home to a thriving community of commercial artists

little more than 14 per cent of the total population and numbers are set to rise. In fact, native Ibizans now account for less than 50 per cent of islanders, the remainder comprising migrants from the Spanish mainland and seasonal workers from Ecuador and Morocco who are employed in the construction and service industries. It is a moot point whether Ibiza is on its way to losing its traditional culture and identity, even its voice. Since 1994 foreign residents have been entitled to vote in municipal elections. So far, relatively few have exercised this right but the signs are that attitudes may be changing. Regional politicians are increasingly sensitive to the needs of foreign constituents who might one day sweep them from office.

Eivissa

Known in Spanish as Pueblo Ibiza (Ibiza Town), the capital of the Pitiusas (population 40,000) is a major tourist attraction, with enough to interest visitors for at least a couple of days. The fortress city of Dalt Vila would rate five stars by any standard. Then there are the quaint fishermen's quarters below the walls and the port with its marinas, restaurants and nightclubs. With the best-conserved Punic burial site in the Mediterranean and at least three beaches nearby, you have all the ingredients for an enjoyable stay.

Eivissa is the ideal base for touring the island. Transport to Santa Eulària, Sant Antoni and the north of the island is excellent and there are regular daily sailings to Formentera (in summer).

Dalt Vila

When Dalt Vila was declared a World Heritage Site by UNESCO in 1999, its almost perfectly preserved Renaissance fortifications were judged to be of 'singular historic, architectural and

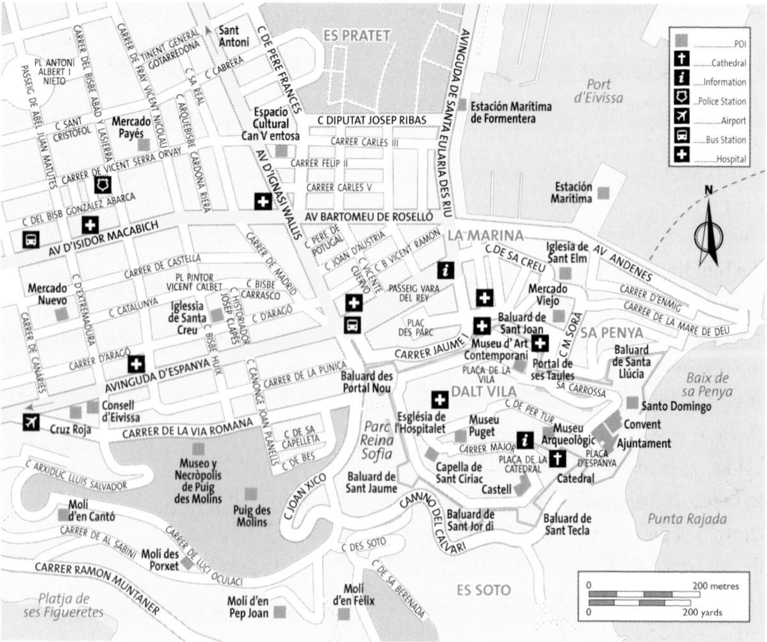

cultural value'. The sights of the Upper Town include the walls and bastions, the cathedral, the castle, a 16th-century monastery (now the town hall), several museums, some splendid mansions dating from the 15th to the 19th centuries, and a number of picturesque squares provided with café terraces, restaurants and gift shops. From almost any point along the walls there are breathtaking views of Eivissa town and bay, the beaches of Figueretes and d'en Bossa, the salt marshes of Ses Salines and the island of Formentera.

Ajuntament (Town Hall)

This 16th-century building was originally a Dominican monastery. The first monks arrived on the island around 1580 and made their headquarters in the parish church at Jesús. A pirate raid prompted second thoughts, and in 1587 they sought the protection of Dalt Vila's newly completed fortress walls. Here they remained until the disentailment of the monasteries in 1835 when the town councillors sent them packing and used the building as a prison, hospital and school, before moving in themselves. The arcaded cloister – all that remains of the original monastery – makes an attractive backdrop for the concerts of classical music and folk dancing displays held here from time to time. Next door to the town hall is the former monastic church, dedicated to **Sant Pere**, although the parishioners insist on calling it Santo Domingo – it is the image of this saint which presides over the high altar. The church dates from 1592, although it was later given a pretty comprehensive Baroque facelift. The red-tiled domes and most of the interior decoration, including the ceiling frescoes and Valencian *azulejos*, are from the later period. Outside the church, Carrer Balansat leads to the **Baluard de Santa Llúcia** and wonderful harbour views. The bastion, sometimes used for concerts, including a mini jazz festival in summer, has recently been restored. It originally contained a gunpowder store, known as **Es Polvorí**, which blew up in 1730 after being struck by lightning, seriously damaging the Dominican monastery nearby.

Església de Sant Pere. Open: only during services (Sat 7pm, Sun noon & 7pm).

Steps on Carrer Conquista, Dalt Vila

Calvi's walls

In the mid-16th century the greatest menace to Christian civilisation and the security of Europe were the Turks. Ottoman armies had already invaded the Balkans and would eventually reach the gates of Vienna. At sea, the reach of the Turkish navy extended from the Aegean Sea to the north coast of Africa, from where its Berber allies launched crippling raids against Christian outposts in the islands of the Mediterranean, not least Ibiza. In 1554 the Habsburg emperor Charles V decided that strengthening Dalt Vila's defences was a matter of urgency, but it was his son and heir, Felipe II, who was to assume responsibility for the task.

The fortifications that were built by the Carthaginians around the 4th century BC, if not quite one of the wonders of the ancient world, won the admiration of contemporaries, and, in 217 BC, the walls withstood a siege by the Roman general Cornelius Scipio. Following the Arab conquest of the Pitiusas in the early 10th century, the defences were extended to encompass the growing city. The walls were rebuilt on three successive levels and surmounted by a keep, the Almudaina. Even though these fortifications were crumbling by the 16th century, it made sense to use them as the foundation for the new defences. Finding the money was the problem. The Spanish monarchy was strapped for cash and Felipe had to turn to the archbishop of Valencia for the initial down payment of 20,000 ducats. When costs spiralled

Calvi's walls have stood the test of time

Cannon could be wheeled from one bastion to another via Calvi's 'ring road'

by more than 150 per cent, the Spaniards raided the salt revenues.

The military engineer hand-picked by the king for the task was a Roman, Giovanni Battista Calvi. Calvi had an impressive track record, including the fortifications at Maó (Menorca), Palma (Mallorca) and Barcelona. His remit in Ibiza extended to the protection of Santa Eulària and the salt pans at Ses Salines. Calvi was assisted by four local master masons: Antoni Jaume, Gaspar Puig, Pere Francesc and Antoni Lobo. They began by constructing six massive pentagonal bastions (*baluardes*), later named Sant Joan, Santa Tecla, Sant Bernat, Sant Jordi, Sant Jaume and Portal Nou. Each was strategically positioned to guard part of the city and given its own garrison. The Berbers had increased their fire power over the years, so each bulwark was cleverly angled to deflect enemy fire. When the need arose, artillery pieces could be moved from one bastion to another along what is now Calvi's ring road (Ronda de Calvi). Work was already well advanced when, in 1575, another Italian engineer, Giovanni Paleazzo Fratin, was brought in to construct an extra bastion to guard the Vila Nova, the 'new town' of Santa Llúcia, after which the corresponding bulwark was named.

By 1585 the defences were complete. Dalt Vila was girdled by walls 5m (16½ft) thick, 25m (82ft) high and 2km (1¼ miles) in length. There is a note of defiance, disdain even, in the elegance of Calvi's design – a confidence bordering on certainty that the defences would never be breached. And they never were. Eivissa was rid of the pirate menace for good.

The eye-catching tiled roof of the Dominican monastery, Dalt Vila

Capella de Sant Ciriac (Chapel of St Ciricac)

Candles often burn before the shrine to St Ciriac, whose feast falls on 8 August, the anniversary of the Catalan invasion in 1235. Peer in, and behind the grille you should see the entrance to a sealed-up tunnel. It was through here that the first of Guillem de Montgrí's forces penetrated the Arab defences – after receiving a tip-off, so the story goes, from the governor's treacherous brother. (They had fallen out over a girl in the harem.) The chapel, completed in 1752, holds an annual service of commemoration when flowers are laid before the image of the saint.
Carrer de Sant Ciriac.

Carrer Major (Main Street)

Dalt Vila's main street is lined with handsome mansions built by the cream of the Catalan aristocracy – or so they claimed when they arrived in Ibiza, later advertising their lineage by carving spurious but highly imaginative coats of arms into the façades of their grand houses. **Can Llaudis** (*No 18*) is rated the finest example of secular Catalan Gothic architecture on the island. Built around an interior courtyard, a Renaissance staircase leads to what were the living quarters on the main floor. Note the crest of the Laudes family, who owned the house before it passed into the hands of the Comasemas, a merchant family from Mallorca, in the

18th century. Can Llaudis used to house paintings by the distinguished Ibizan artist Narcís Puget Viñas (1874–1960). Unfortunately, the humidity damaged the works, which had to be restored in the Archaeological Museum. **Can Balansat** (*No 10*) was the ancestral home of one of Ibiza's most distinguished families – note the 16th-century windows. **Torre del Canónigo** (*No 8*), now a hotel, is built on medieval foundations that conceal an Arab cistern.

Carrer de Per Tur

Retired corsairs who had made their fortune defending Ibiza's honour on the high seas were among the owners of the mansions that grace this street. Look out particularly for **Can Montero** (*No 1*), a 17th-century building originally owned by a Genoese family of merchants. **Can Mariano Tur** (*No 3*) dates from the 18th century, **Can Llobet** (*No 7*) from the 19th century and **Casa Verdera** (*No 6*) from the 17th century. Just at the end of Carrer de Per Tur, on Carrer Joan Roman (*No 2*), is the **Antic Seminari**, which the Jesuits made their headquarters from 1669 until the order was expelled from Spain in 1767. This 'des res' has been converted into luxury apartments.

Castell (Castle)

The castle guards the summit of Dalt Vila, occupying the rock on which the city was founded more than 2,600 years ago. Excavations beneath the site have yielded the remains of dwellings from the Punic period, and wells from the time of the Moorish occupation. The castle incorporates what remains of the Arab fortress known as the *Almudaina*, where the governor of Yebisah (the Arabic name for Ibiza) resided. The buildings have been remodelled on a number of occasions, most recently in the 18th century when the castle was used as a barracks. An access staircase was added in 1993, and the castle has been extensively restored. Although not currently open to the public, it can be seen from the outside.

Catedral (Cathedral)

Before setting out on their historic mission to conquer Ibiza, Guillem de Montgrí and his followers made a solemn vow that, should they be successful, they would build a church dedicated to the Virgin. 'Our Lady

Close-up view of Dalt Vila castle

of the Snows' may not be the most obvious patroness for a sunny island but her feast day occurs on 5 August, conveniently close to the anniversary of the invasion. This site has been a place of worship since the city was founded. The Carthaginians built a temple to the god Eshmun here in the 7th century. The Romans followed suit and, when the Moors arrived, they built a mosque over the ruins, which the Catalans later consecrated for Christian worship.

The cathedral bell tower is a Dalt Vila landmark

Work on the new cathedral began early in the 14th century but dragged on for over 200 years. The project was financed partly by profits from the lucrative salt trade. Only the side chapels, the sacristy and the bell tower are in the Catalan Gothic style. The rest of the building was given an insensitive makeover in the 18th century by a group of Valencian architects, including Pere Ferrer, who built the parish church in Sant Josep (*see p106*). The best of the artwork, including 15th-century paintings by Francesc Gomes and a retable attributed to Valentí Montiliu, may eventually find its way to the Museu Diocesà (Diocesan Museum – *see p42*). *Open: Mon–Sat 10am–1.30pm & 4–7pm. Not for visits during Sunday mass 10.30am. Free admission.*

Església de l'Hospitalet (Church of Sta Maria de Gràcia)

Near the old seminary on the corner of Sant Josep and Santa Fac is the plain, whitewashed façade of a 15th-century hospital for the poor. The church dates from 1423 and was the focal point of the small community who lived here – a special viewing balcony was built so that the sick patients could see the priest saying Mass. This was also the seat of the Confraternity of the Blood, a lay brotherhood, whose duties included accompanying condemned prisoners to the scaffold. The Església de l'Hospitalet is now a cultural centre and is occasionally used for art exhibitions.

Museu Arqueològic d'Eivissa i Formentera (Archaeological Museum)

The Archaeological Museum has a modest but interesting collection of prehistoric, Phoenician, Roman and Islamic artefacts, spanning nearly 3,000 years of Ibizan history. The big disappointment is the Punic collection, most of which is now in the sister museum at the Puig des Molins site (*see p54*). The displays are arranged chronologically in half a dozen well-lit rooms. All the items are clearly labelled in English as well as Spanish. The finds, from excavations across the Pitiusas, include prehistoric bone tools and axe heads, pottery, jewellery, glassware, coins and statuary. The period of the Phoenician colonisation is well represented, with perfume bottles from Italy, Egyptian scarabs and Spanish amphorae, reflecting the wide commercial and cultural reach of this great seafaring people. Look out for the originals of the statues guarding Ses Taules, Roman coins with the image of the Emperor on one side and the Punic goddess Tanit (Bes) on the other, and some of the earthenware figures of Tanit discovered in the sanctuary at Es Cuieram. The museum occupies a number of buildings of historic importance. At the core is the 15th-century headquarters of the Universitat, the body that governed the Pitiusas from 1299 to 1715. The **Capella del Salvador**, now the reception area, has a splendid 14th-century vaulted ceiling.

Gothic ceiling of the Capella del Salvador, now part of the Archaeological Museum

The chapel was occupied by the seamen's guild until 1702. Part of the exhibition is located in the **Baluard de Santa Tecla**, from where there are wonderful harbour views. Visitors can also see part of the 14th-century fortifications through a glass panel in the floor. The museum shop sells postcards and reproductions but no glossy publications. A free explanatory leaflet with ground plan is available in English and other languages.

Open: mid-Mar–mid-Oct Tue–Sat 10am–2pm & 6–8pm, Sun 10am–2pm; mid-Oct–mid-Mar Tue–Sat 9am–3pm. Admission charge.

Museu d'Art Contemporani d'Eivissa (Contemporary Art Museum)
This museum is housed in the Baluard de Sant Joan, immediately to the right of Portal de ses Taules. It was originally used as an arsenal and armoury. The museum was founded in 1966 when artists from as far afield as the United States and Japan, as well as Western Europe, formed a close community on the island, seduced by the landscape and the bohemian lifestyle in equal measure. Their work is now on display here, alongside that of Ibizan and Spanish contemporaries. Keep an eye out for temporary exhibitions.
Open: May–Oct Tue–Sun 10am–1.30pm & 5–8pm; Nov–Apr Tue–Sun 10am–1.30pm & 4–6pm. Admission charge.

Museu Diocesà (Diocesan Museum)
Also known as the **Museu de la Catedral**, the collection comprises all kinds of sacred art, from religious paintings and enamels to jewel-encrusted vestments and gleaming gold and silver plate. One of the museum's prize possessions is a monstrance made in Mallorca in the late 14th or early 15th century.
Open: Mon–Sat 10am–1.30pm & 4–7pm. Admission charge.

Plaça de la Catedral
In the Middle Ages the buildings around this square were occupied by the island's institutions of government. On the corner of Carrer Major is the **Reial Curia**, where the judges and notaries had their offices. The Gothic

The Contemporary Art Museum was founded in 1966

Enjoy lunch on the terrace in Plaça de la Vila

door beneath the tower was originally a window. The coat of arms belongs to Felipe V, the Spanish monarch responsible for abolishing Ibiza's autonomy in the 18th century. Next door to the Reial Curia is the Museu Arqueològic d'Eivissa i Formentera.

GETTING THE BEST FROM DALT VILA

Get hold of a copy of the free large-scale street map from the tourist office. Take your time – Dalt Vila is for savouring. Avoid the afternoon crush and come early in the morning when you'll find it easier to negotiate the engaging labyrinth of lanes, alleyways, ramps and stairways out of the heat of the sun. Return for a romantic stroll after dark when the precincts are illuminated and the atmosphere is hushed and relaxed. Perhaps round off the experience with a meal in El Olivo or one of the other fine restaurants on Plaça de la Vila and Sa Carrossa.

Plaça d'Espanya

At the centre of this cobbled square, shaded by palm trees, is a monument to Guillem de Montgrí, the aristocratic archbishop of Tarragona who led the conquering Catalan-Aragonese expedition in 1235 and administered part of the island thereafter, albeit *in absentia.* Given Montgrí's martial credentials, it seems almost perverse to present him in a recumbent posture, as here, rather than on horseback.

Plaça de la Vila

While only just inside the fortress walls, Plaça de la Vila is the real heart of the Upper Town, where cafés, boutiques, art galleries and exclusive restaurants draw large crowds to the terraces outside the square's simple,

(*Cont. on p46*)

The Carthaginian heritage

During the 1st century BC the Roman geographer Diodorus Siculus wrote of 'ports worthy of mention, great walls, as well as a considerable number of admirably built houses. Foreigners of all classes live there, mostly Phoenicians.' He was describing the Carthaginian colony of Ibosim (Eivissa), founded, according to tradition, in 654 BC. Carthage was itself a Phoenician colony, dating from the 9th century BC. The Phoenicians were a seafaring people, originally from what is now Lebanon. They were traders rather than empire builders, and they established outposts all over the Mediterranean. However, by the end of the 6th century BC, the Carthaginians had outgrown Phoenician tutelage and were building their own network of colonies along the coast of North Africa, in Andalucía, Sicily, Sardinia and southern France. In the process they created a distinctive Punic civilisation (the name derives from their dialect).

To the Carthaginians, Ibiza was a natural resource to be exploited. The original Phoenician settlement of Sa Caleta was abandoned in favour of Ibosim, a large, natural harbour which became an important strategic point in the western Mediterranean, a nexus of trading routes. They fortified the city walls and built a settlement on the hillside of Dalt Vila down to the shoreline, where evidence of shops and houses has been discovered. A cluster of ceramic workshops suggests that an artisanal quarter existed near what is now

Ancient tombs in the necropolis at Puig des Molins

Clay statuettes of the Carthaginian deities

Avinguda d'Espanya. The Carthaginians capitalised on the salt pans at Ses Salines and they mined silver and lead at S'Argentera (*minium*, a red oxide extract, was used for painting pottery). More lucrative was the export of a purple pigment derived from whelks and used to dye Roman togas. Ibizan pine forests were an important source of wood for Carthage's shipbuilders. Even most of the crops (cereals, figs, olives and fruit) found their way overseas. Able-bodied islanders were hired as mercenaries, acquiring a fearsome reputation as sling-throwers. Ibiza thrived. The island minted its own coins and industrial production increased. Amphorae, used for transporting rough wines and oils, have been found in many parts of the Mediterranean. But the greatest trawl of artefacts has been unearthed on Puig des Molins: vases, coins, necklaces and amulets, terracotta figurines, polychrome ostrich eggs and surgical instruments.

Puig des Molins (*see p54*) was a highly prized place of burial, because of the absence of poisonous snakes and marauding animals – a prerequisite for a necropolis. Wealthy Carthaginians from all over the empire paid handsomely to have their bodies interred here. The site's religious significance can be appreciated from the large number of effigies of Punic deities. By far the most important of these was Tanit, goddess of love and fertility. Her symbols included doves, palm trees, grapes and the crescent moon. No evidence has been found, however, of the Carthaginian practice of child sacrifice, attested to again by Diodorus Siculus.

Finally at rest – monument to the turbulent crusading knight Guillem de Montgrí in Plaça d'Espanya

whitewashed frontages. During the day, visitors are entertained by fire eaters and flamenco dancers, but after dark, when the square is illuminated, it has a still, magical quality even though many of the shops remain open. Just off Plaça de la Vila is the **Baluard de Sant Joan**. From the garden there are views of La Marina and the harbour.

Portal de ses Taules

Visitors enter Dalt Vila through the magnificent 16th-century portcullis, a typical Renaissance set piece. Above the Gate of the Tablets is a carving in stone relief of the Habsburg coat of arms of Felipe II of Spain. The Latin inscription on the tablet underneath praises his achievements and recalls the official completion of the fortifications in 1584. In niches flanking the gateway are two headless marble statues, copied from Roman originals and recovered by a military engineer during the construction of the fortress. One represents the goddess Juno, the other a Roman soldier. The drawbridge spanning the dried-up moat looks the part but is actually a replica of the original and was installed only in 1990. Inside the gateway is the colonnaded **Pati d'Armes**, a courtyard-cum-guardroom where soldiers warmed themselves on chilly winter nights at the open hearth near the entrance. The doorway at the end is decorated with the coat of arms of Catalunya and Aragón. After the rebuilding of Dalt Vila in the 16th century, the Pati d'Armes served as the town market.

Sa Carrossa

The carriages that passed along this important thoroughfare in days gone by gave it its name. At the centre of the street is a bronze bust of the Ibizan historian, poet and priest Isidor Macabich (1883–1973). Just about every town on the island has a street commemorating this important local figure, descended from a family of Croatian merchants. Macabich began life as a journalist on the *Diario de Ibiza*. After his ordination in 1907, he was appointed Cathedral archivist, a post he held for many years. He is the author of numerous historical works, culminating in a definitive four-volume *History of Ibiza*, which appeared in the 1960s. Near the statue is a eucalyptus tree, which inspired some of his verses. Of the bars, coffee shops and restaurants on Sa Carrossa, La Muralla (right at the top) is popular with gay visitors, who meet here before heading off to the Anfora nightclub (*see p103*).

Vila Nova

The 'New Town' is approached via Dalt Vila's only surviving Arab gateway, **Sa Portela**. (Look for the left turn shortly after Carrer Sant Ciriac becomes Carrer Major.) The New Town includes Plaça d'Espanya, Plaça de la Vila and the Baluard de Santa Llúcia, the last of the bastions to be completed.

On Carrer de Santa Maria is the El Corsario hotel, where the last of Ibiza's great privateers, Antoni Riquer, lived in the early 19th century.

The Pati d'Armes has a charm of its own

Walk: Exploring Dalt Vila

This walk introduces you to Dalt Vila, Eivissa's stunning walled town, declared a World Heritage Site by UNESCO. Along the way to the Gothic cathedral and the castle at the summit are splendid noblemen's houses and tiny irregular plaças *lined with restaurants, boutiques and café terraces. The walk requires only a moderate amount of stamina, although there are quite a few steep steps to negotiate.*

Allow 3 hours.

The starting point is the main entrance at Portal de ses Taules.

1 Portal de ses Taules

Two Roman statues preside over either side of the gate; one represents a Roman soldier, the other, Juno, queen of the gods and the Roman equivalent of the Punic goddess Tanit. Above the entrance is the coat of arms of the Habsburg dynasty, to which Felipe II of Spain belonged. Cross the drawbridge

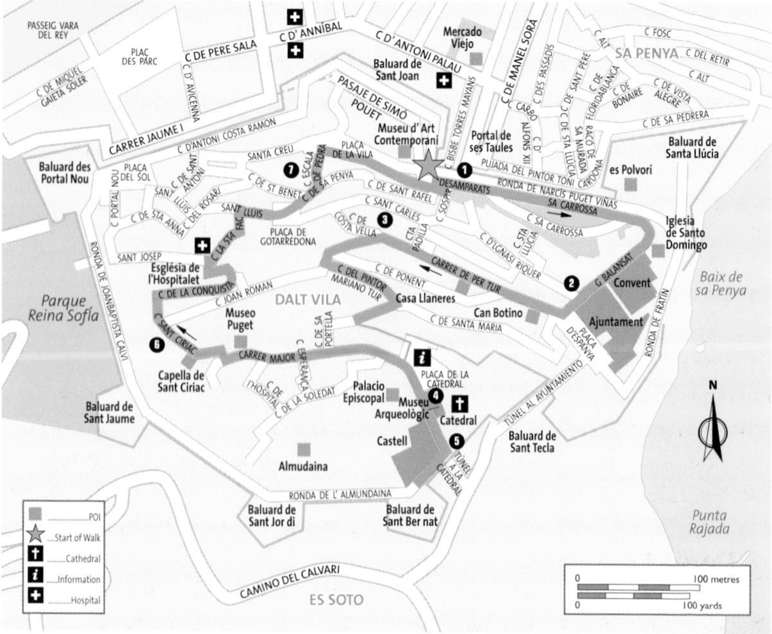

to the Pati d'Armes, an arched courtyard that served as a kind of guardroom. The smaller gateway at the end leads in to Plaça de la Vila.

2 Ajuntament (Town Hall)

Turn left onto Sa Carrossa to the Baroque church of Santo Domingo and the former Dominican monastery, which is now the Town Hall. Turn onto Plaça d'Espanya and look out from the ravelin to the lighthouse across the bay on the Botafoc Peninsula.

3 Streets of the old town

Make the gentle ascent up Carrer de Per Tur, a street lined with historic mansions. When you reach the Antic Seminari, cross Carrer Joan Roman and climb the steps past the legendary El Corsario hotel, once a pirates' den. Cross Carrer de Santa Maria and take the next flight of steps on the left to Carrer Major. On your right you will see the Gothic doorway of the Reial Curia, where Ibizan justice was dispensed in the Middle Ages.

4 Museu Arqueològic

On the left is the Archaeological Museum. Located in historic buildings adjoining the Baluard de Santa Tecla, it has an interesting collection of Punic and Roman artefacts found in various sites on Ibiza and Formentera.

5 Catedral and Castell

Cross Plaça de la Catedral to the cathedral (open to the public) and the Diocesan Museum. Behind the cathedral is the Baluard de Sant Bernat, which offers panoramic views of the town, harbour and surrounding countryside. Now turn round and look at the castle. Although it was heavily restored in the 18th century, you can still make out a rectangular tower which was part of the original Almudaina, or Moorish keep.

Dalt Vila is best explored on foot

6 Sant Ciriac

Return via Carrer Major, Dalt Vila's 'high street', which leads into Carrer Sant Ciriac.

7 Plaça de la Vila

Take the steps down to Carrer de la Conquista, past the El Palacio hotel. At the end, turn right, passing the whitewashed walls of the 15th-century Església de l'Hospitalet, to Sant Lluis, then left down Escala de Pedra. At the bottom is Plaça de la Vila, with its lively café terraces and restaurants.

Extramuros (beyond the walls)

Until the beginning of the 19th century, Eivissa was confined to Dalt Vila and the two medieval neighbourhoods of La Marina and Sa Penya. This changed with the creation of Vara de Rey, an elegant boulevard only a few minutes' walk from Puig des Molins. This is the one 'must see' in the modern town, sometimes referred to as The Extension (*s'Eixample*). Most visitors get no further than the bus station on Avinguda d'Isidor Macabich, although the New Town is a good place to get to know the locals. The prices are lower here, too.

La Marina

Immediately below the walls of Dalt Vila, in the shadow of the Baluard de Sant Joan, is the old fishermen's quarter, now crammed with restaurants, bars, souvenir shops and fashion boutiques, open day and night and geared almost exclusively to the tourist market. To the east of the ramp leading to Ses Taules is the fish market (**Mercat des Peix**), an octagonal building dating from 1875. Also worth a look is the old fruit and vegetable market (**Mercat Vell**) on Plaça de sa Constitució, a handsome structure with a façade of Doric columns. The locals fight shy of paying the high prices here, preferring the unromantic new market on Carrer d'Extremadura. You could stop for a coffee in one of the cafés on the square or move on to the 19th-century **Teatro Pereira** on Carrer Comte Rosello. No longer a theatre, it is now an important venue for jazz concerts and other musical events. The foyer doubles as a café.

Església de Sant Elm on Carrer de sa Creu, with a tiered bell tower, was the church of the guild of seafarers and ships' carpenters (*open only for services*). The original chapel was razed to the ground by pirates in 1578, just before the new town defences were completed. On 16 July La Marina's fishermen honour a centuries-old tradition by sailing into the harbour with a statue of the Virgin and Child from the church.

Boat excursions to nearby beaches depart from the **Estació Marítima** building on the waterfront. The obelisk here commemorates the last of the

ANTONI RIQUER ARABÍ (1773–1846)

Born in La Marina, Riquer went to sea at an early age and quickly established a reputation for skilful seamanship among his fellow corsairs. Officially credited with capturing no fewer than 100 French and British vessels, his greatest exploit occurred in 1806 when, against overwhelming odds, he overpowered a 250-tonne British brig, the *Felicity*, in full view of patriotic locals gathered on the quayside. A bit of a romantic, on hearing in 1831 that the Spanish general Torrijos had been captured after leading a coup against the reactionary ruler Fernando VII, Riquer attempted to free him from the prison in Malaga where he was being held. After Torrijos was executed, Riquer himself was accused of treason, but pardoned in view of his valuable services to the Spanish crown.

View of La Marina

great Ibizan corsairs, Antoni Riquer Arabí (*see box opposite*).

Sa Penya

La Marina leads without interruption to Sa Penya, another historic quarter of red-roofed, whitewashed houses. Gaze down on it from the Baluard de Santa Llucia and it will become clear why this precariously sited working-class neighbourhood is called 'the crag'. A picturesque warren of cobbled passages and steep alleyways accessed by stone staircases, Sa Penya also profits from tourism. The bars and boutiques along Carrer de la Mare de Déu are especially popular with gay visitors, although everyone is welcome. Stick to the well-lit areas at night, as Sa Penya has a reputation for crime and drug dealing.

Passeig de Vara del Rey

This handsome boulevard, completed in 1912, was designed by the Mallorcan architect Josep Aloner. The focal point is a monument to the Ibizan general Joaquin Vara del Rey, killed in action in 1898 during the disastrous war with the

(*Cont. on p54*)

Pirates and corsairs

Head in the direction of the tourist office in Eivissa and you will come across a stone obelisk known as The Monument to the Privateers. It commemorates the Ibizan corsairs who for centuries fought off foreign pirate attacks, defending the islanders as well as the possessions of the Catalan and Spanish crowns. The most famous of these swashbuckling heroes, Antoni Riquer Arabí (1773–1846), is honoured in the adjacent square (*see p50*). Corsairs first assumed their roles as guardian angels in the 14th century. As the war chest of the local authority, the Universitat, was simply too small to organise its own military expeditions, the Catalan government began issuing registration certificates. The holders of these had a powerful incentive: capture an enemy pirate vessel and four-fifths of the plunder is yours. Not surprisingly, there was no shortage of volunteers, and this lucrative form of private enterprise became big business.

The corsairs had a fearsome reputation, but so did the enemy. For more than 300 years, the main threat to the islands came from the Barbary states of the North African coast, where the pirates were given carte blanche to harass the Christian populations of the Mediterranean. Setting out from Tripoli, Tunis and Algiers, they used hit-and-run tactics, arriving in fleets of up to 20 ships, briefly occupying a weakly

Once a pirates' den, El Corsario is now a hotel

defended port before sacking the town and beating a hasty retreat. Any inhabitants they didn't murder, they took prisoner for ransom or to be sold into slavery. The secret weapon of the Barbary pirates was the *jabeque*. A pinewood vessel with a sleek hull and three sails, it was light, quick and easy to manoeuvre. When cannons were fitted in the 17th century, the *jabeque* became virtually invincible.

Alarmed by the growth of Turkish power in the Mediterranean (the Turks and the Barbary states were allies), and the devastating impact on commerce, the Christian rulers of western Europe were finally spurred into action. In 1554, the year in which the dreaded pirate-admiral Barbarossa destroyed Maó harbour in Menorca, Carlos I of Spain authorised the rebuilding of Eivissa's defences. His son, Felipe II, was entrusted with overseeing the work, both here and in Santa Eulària, which had only recently succumbed to a devastating pirate attack. Subsequently, a system of watchtowers, known as *atalayas*, from the Arab word for sentinel, was established to protect the coastline. These huge bastions were manned by *talaiers*, watchmen who, on spotting an enemy vessel out at sea, lit a warning fire (smoke by day) to alert the neighbouring tower, which duly passed on the message. Forewarned, the peasants in the surrounding countryside would head for the safety of the newly fortified churches, where the defenders were concentrated.

The Monument to the Privateers is a waterfront landmark in Eivissa

By the mid-17th century, the corsairs were finally gaining the upper hand, thanks to the development of the *jabeque-polacra*, a much larger and better armed version of the Berber prototype. The naval defeat of the Turks at Lepanto in 1571 staved off the Ottoman threat. The improved island defences were also a deterrent, to the extent that in 1697 the decision was taken to recolonise Formentera, which had been uninhabited for centuries. In 1828 the corsair fleets were officially disbanded. Two years later, the French occupied Algiers and the Barbary pirates lost their main base in North Africa. At last, the people of Ibiza could live in peace.

Palm-lined promenade, Platja des Figueretes

United States in which Spain lost the last of her overseas colonies. Vara de Rey's heroic exploits at El Caney, Cuba, when he led his troops against overwhelming odds before falling to an enemy bullet, captured the popular imagination. The statue was paid for by public subscription and there is even a square named after the general in Madrid. Vara del Rey is where the locals buy their newspapers in the morning, returning later in the day for the traditional *paseo* (evening stroll) and a drink on one of the café terraces. For that reason, tables are at a premium – get there before 9pm if you do not want to be disappointed. Alternatively, try the cafés on **Plaça des Parc**, the shady, traffic-free square to the south. There you can admire the neoclassical town houses from the small terrace outside the Sunset Café, which serves excellent breakfasts to a faithful clientele of Ibizans and foreign residents.

Platja des Figueretes

This small suburban beach, encroached on by apartment blocks and hotels, is just 15 minutes' walk from Eivissa town centre. Crowds are guaranteed on the sands during the summer months, but the palm-shaded promenade makes for a pleasant stroll at this or any other time of year. There are views of Dalt Vila to be enjoyed from the car park on Carrer Ramon Muntaner.

Puig des Molins

The best-preserved Punic cemetery discovered to date contains as many as 4,000 tombs from all points in the Mediterranean. It was chosen specifically because Ibiza was free of poisonous snakes and other creatures harmful to man. The burial chambers were looted as a matter of course until well into the 20th century. Even so, the finds – amulets, necklaces, gold collars, funeral masks, mirrors, painted ostrich eggs, amphorae and much more besides – are extraordinary and attest to the prosperity of this intriguing civilisation. A nine-storey museum (Museu Monografic) was built alongside the site to house the exhibits. Visitors are allowed onto the site to see one of the chambers which contains around a

dozen stone sarcophagi. The Department of Culture organises free guided tours of Puig des Molins and the mill at Des Porxet (ask at the tourist office for more details).
Puig des Molins, Via Romana 13. Open: mid-Mar–mid-Oct Tue–Sat 10am–2pm & 6–8pm, Sun 10am–2pm; mid-Oct–mid-Mar Tue–Sat 9am–3pm, Sun 10am–2pm.

Platja d'en Bossa

During the summer there are regular ferry services from Eivissa to this unashamedly brash, overdeveloped resort where the main attraction is the longest sandy beach on the island – 3km (2 miles) – with not much in the way of shade but excellent watersports facilities. Apart from families with children, Platja d'en Bossa's biggest fans are the clubbers, who usually head straight for the Space dance club (open all day). Strung out along the back of the resort is a seemingly endless line of pubs, supermarkets and fast-food outlets. It is hardly an oasis of peace and quiet then, even without the roar of engines as aircraft make their descent to the airport. Just inland from the beach is the church of **Sant Jordi de ses Salines**, its crenellated walls a reminder that this was once an integral part of the defensive system that guarded the salt pans (*see pp118–19*). Sant Jordi is one of the oldest religious foundations on the island, dating from shortly after the Catalan Conquest. The present church was erected in 1577 and restored in the 19th century. If you happen to be here on a Saturday, you could call in at the flea market, which is held in the hippodrome, a former venue for trotting races. The market is open all year round.

Port d'Eivissa

The harbour district begins just north of La Marina, on Avinguda Santa Eulària des Riu, and is best explored on foot. Almost every visitor to the island will become acquainted, with the Formentera ferry terminal (**Estación Maritima dé Formentera**), a couple of minutes' walk from the tourist office and only a stone's throw from the **Club Nàutic** (Yacht Club). Beyond the roundabout at the start of Passeig de Joan Carles I is the **Casino** and, just inland, the turning for Pacha, Ibiza's oldest nightclub. Pacha's rival, El Divino, enjoys a superb setting overlooking the **Marina Botafoc**, with its shops, restaurants and boutiques. Behind the main road is the protected land of **Ses Feixes**, first farmed by the Moors in the 10th century (*see p58*). Continue along Passeig de Joan Carles I to the **Botafoc Peninsula**, three small islets now joined together by a roadway. The remains of a Punic cemetery were discovered on Illa Plana, where plague victims were quarantined during the Middle Ages. Guarding the approaches to the harbour is the 300-year-old Botafoc lighthouse, from where there are outstanding views of Dalt Vila and the old quarters of Eivissa.

Drive: From Eivissa

This drive sets out from the island's capital to explore the delightful villages and coves of the east and northeast coasts, before returning to Eivissa, via the rolling green hills of the Ibizan interior. The round trip, which includes some steep winding roads, is about 90km (60 miles).

Allow one day to enjoy the places to the full.

1 Santa Eulària des Riu

Leave Eivissa on the C-733 heading north. After 6km (4 miles), turn right onto the road to Santa Eulària. On your right is Roca Llisa, Ibiza's 18-hole golf course, and a series of turnings to the stunning beach at Cala Llonga. Stop in Santa Eulària to visit the fortified hilltop church to the west of the modern town.

2 Sant Carles de Peralta

The next stop on the road north (6km/4 miles from Santa Eulària) is the sleepy village of Sant Carles. In the 1960s this was one of the hippies' favourite haunts – one or two of them still patronise Anita's bar, a good place to stop for coffee and a snack.

3 Two diversions

A side road leads from the centre of Sant Carles to the sheltered cove of Cala Mastella. The calm, clear waters of the pine-clad inlet are a good reason for a swim. Hidden by the rocks is a sought-after *chiringuito*, Bigotes, famous for freshly caught fish. An alternative to Cala Mastella is to leave Sant Carles in the direction of Cala Sant Vicent. Turn right after 1km (1/2 mile) to the small fishing hamlet of Pou d'es Lleó, where the rock-strewn sands are usually deserted. Either route is an attractive drive, passing through terraced olive groves and citrus orchards.

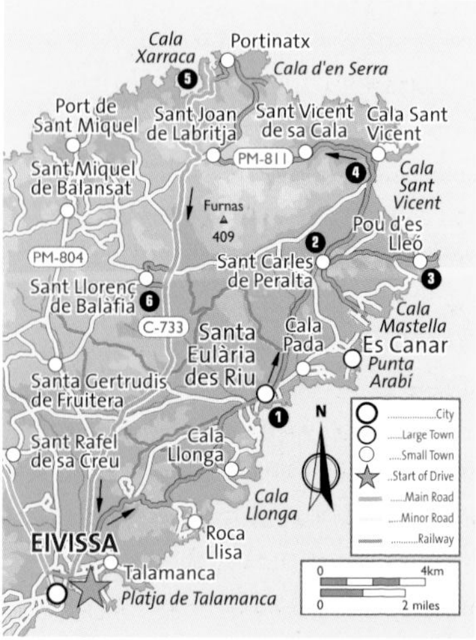

A fishing boat near Cala Mastella

4 The road to Cala Sant Vicent

Follow the PM-810 road north from Sant Carles for 2km (1¼ miles), and this road will then run by the coast at Cala Sant Vicent. There are spectacular cliff-top views as the road emerges from the pine forest.

5 Portinatx

Turn left when you arrive in Cala Sant Vicent and follow the road as it climbs up through a beautiful valley to Ibiza's smallest village, Sant Vicent de sa Cala. The tortuous ascent continues into the Serra Grossa and the municipal centre of Sant Joan de Labritja. Take a right turn here onto another beautiful stretch of road, which winds through the forest down to the sea. As you approach Portinatx, look out for the emerald waters of Cala d'en Serra off to your right. The secluded beach is a 1.5km (1-mile) walk away – follow the very rough track. You may be tempted to stop for a meal in the *chiringuito* here – the surroundings will be quieter than in the busy resort of Portinatx.

6 Sant Llorenç de Balàfia

Leaving Portinatx, the C-733 skirts the cliff tops, offering fantastic views of Cala Xarraca before turning inland through a typical Ibizan valley of terraced fields, planted with olive groves and citrus trees. At the junction with the road from Sant Joan, turn away from the village (right) and continue along the main road to Eivissa. After 5km (3 miles) the defence towers of Balàfia come into view. Originally a Moorish settlement, the defences were to protect the villagers from pirates. Continue on the C-733 south to return to Eivissa.

Jesús

Barely 2km ($1^1/_4$ miles) northeast of Eivissa on the Cala Llonga road, this suburb is named after the church of Nostra Mare de Jesús. Founded in 1466, it was taken over by the Franciscans when building was still ongoing, some 30 years later. (The Dominicans built a monastery in Jesús later in the 16th century, but moved within a few years to Dalt Vila.)

Nostra Mare de Jesús stands almost alone among Ibizan churches in preserving an artistic treasure throughout the traumatic period of the Civil War. The Gothic altarpiece, in the Flemish tradition, dates from around 1498 and is the work of the Valencian artists Rodrigo de Osona the Younger and Pere Cabanes. In the main panel, the Virgin is portrayed suckling the child Jesus, while a pair of angels sing their praises. Note the panel above, where St Francis of Assisi exhibits the bloody signs of the stigmata, a clear indication that the work was commissioned by the Franciscans. There is little else to detain you in Jesús, apart from a few roadside bars and the Croissanterie Jesús, which serves breakfast to exhausted party-goers on their way home from the Privilege and Amnesia nightclubs.

Església de Nostra Mare de Jesús.
Open: Mon–Sat 10am–1.30pm.

Platja de Talamanca

Just to the north of Eivissa, Talamanca bay is hidden from view by the Botafoc lighthouse. The 2km ($1^1/_4$-mile) long strip of fine, white sand attracts fewer visitors than one might expect, given its proximity to the town, and the beach is freer of development than its rivals to the south, though there are plenty of places to eat and drink. The promenade makes for a pleasant stroll – if you have binoculars you can home in on the sleek yachts that often anchor here in preference to Eivissa. Watersports enthusiasts will want to check out the windsurfing school.

If Talamanca does not appeal, pick up the track at the back of the beach and head for the secluded cove of Cala Roja, just beyond the headland at Cap Martinet. The name 'Rocky Cove' fits the bill perfectly, but this is an idyllic spot for a swim, with a little bit of shade from the pines clinging precariously to the cliff. If the idea of a 2km ($1^1/_4$-mile) walk sounds

SES FEIXES

This area of wetland near Talamanca beach was drained and farmed by the Moors more than 1,000 years ago. Masters of agricultural technology, they created a highly sophisticated irrigation system of dykes, lock gates and water channels, enabling them to grow cabbages, onions and other crops to provide food for the town. Ses Feixes (literally 'The Plots') remained under cultivation until the first wave of package tourists began arriving in the early 1960s. An important bird sanctuary, the entire marsh was declared an 'area of special ecological interest', although this classification has now been challenged by Eivissa town council, which wants to allow limited urban development on the land.

Dalt Vila, reflected in the waters of the Botafoc marina

excessive you could take the hourly bus from Eivissa (summer only) – pack a picnic and make a day of it.

Sant Rafel de sa Creu

The hamlet of Sant Rafel occupies a green hillock 7km (4 miles) from Eivissa on the road to Sant Antoni (*see map p104*). There are stunning views of Dalt Vila (and most of the southern coast) from the 18th-century church. A few restaurants and bars can be found in the village. Sant Rafel's other claim to fame is its many roadside pottery workshops. You will find them along the village high street – the old Sant Antoni road – no more than a five-minute walk from the church.

Church open only for services.

Santa Eulària and the east

Ibiza's third-largest town, Santa Eulària des Riu is beautifully situated in a serene bay, bounded by gently sloping, pine-forested hills. The fortified hill settlement of Puig d'en Missa is a must-see. Santa Eulària is an excellent base for excursions to other parts of the island. Boats leave from the harbour for the famous Hippy Market at Es Canar and the beaches of Cala Pada and Cala Llonga. There are regular bus services to Eivissa and Sant Antoni, but only one a day to Sant Carles.

Cala Llonga and Sol d'en Serra

Seven kilometres (4 miles) south of Santa Eulària, in a narrow inlet sheltered on two sides by towering pine-clad cliffs, is the insensitively developed mini-resort of Cala Llonga. Its setting is as magnificent as its beach, a 200m (656ft) sweep of fine, white sand. The water, unruffled and almost translucent, is perfect for swimming. There's no shade, though, so bring plenty of sunblock and hire a beach umbrella if you don't have one of your own. Watersports available include windsurfing, water-skiing and parasailing – there's also a diving school. Eating and drinking isn't a problem either, in a resort boasting half a dozen restaurants and a couple of *chiringuitos*.

If the crowds begin to pall, it's a pleasant stroll from Cala Llonga to the shingle-and-pebble beach at Sol d'en Serra. Turn right at the La Criolla restaurant, then follow the road until it becomes a bumpy dirt track. Signs from here will point you in the direction of the bay, less than 1km (½ mile) away. The views of Formentera are the main draw – enjoy them from the terrace of the Sol d'en Serra café-restaurant.

Es Canar

The weekly 5km (3-mile) excursion from Santa Eulària to the Hippy Market at Es Canar is one of the most popular on the island. The absence of genuine hippies – the flower children who sold their wares here in the 1970s have long gone – and the fact that authentic, locally made items are not easily come by, will disappoint the purists. For everyone else there's plenty of fun to be had browsing the several hundred stalls in search of that elusive present or holiday souvenir. Kaftans, floppy hats, batik sarongs, leather moccasins, trinkets and watches, bongos and tom-toms, you'll find them all here. If you do intend to buy, bring cash as few stallholders accept

credit cards. The market is near the centre of the resort, in the grounds of the Club Punta Arabí holiday complex on the Carretera Es Canar. You can get there by bus or car, though driving is not advisable in July and August, when the roads are clogged with traffic and parking can be a problem. A more relaxing option is to take the ferry from Santa Eulària. One reason to linger in Es Canar is the Blue Flag beach, a crescent of fine yellow sand, gently shelving and safe for swimming. The small harbour, though, is hemmed in by hotels and apartment blocks, and the bars and restaurants are unenticing.
Hippy Market. Open: Apr–Oct Wed 8am–6pm; bus from Santa Eulària or ferry (May–Oct).

Pine-covered cliffs shelter the magnificent beach at Cala Llonga

Walk: A stroll from Santa Eulària

To get the most out of this 6km (4-mile) walk, take your time and fit in a swim or perhaps a cup of coffee along the way. The route follows a well-worn coastal path from Santa Eulària, ending up in the family resort of Es Canar, best known for its Hippy Market.

Allow 2 hours.

1 Santa Eulària des Riu

Start by walking along the attractive promenade at the back of Santa Eulària's beach and continue on the path which leads towards the cliffs.

2 Punta de s'Església Vella

From 'Old Church Point' there are superb views back towards the marina and the modern town and also across Santa Eulària bay in the direction of

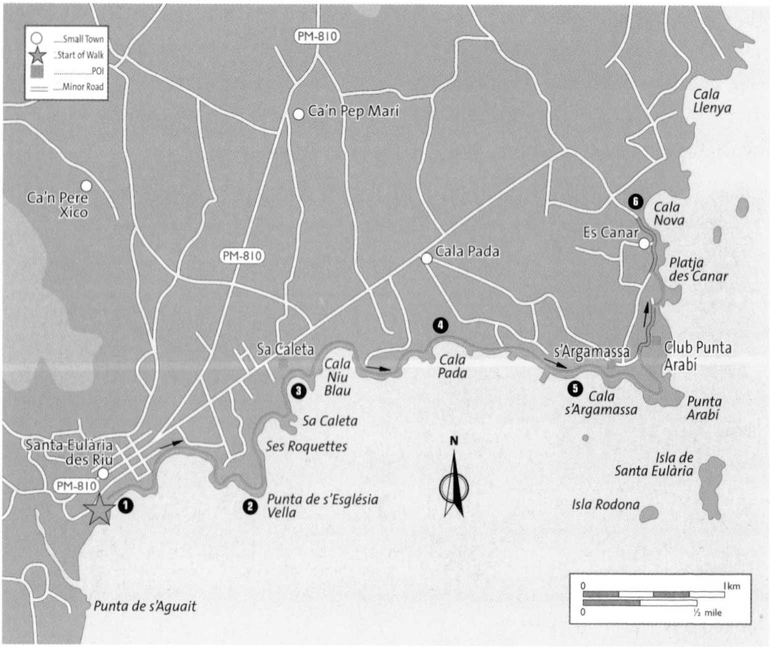

Punta de s'Aguait. The church, though, has long since disappeared. The path now skirts the multi-storey Los Loros Hotel on the way to the bay known as Ses Roquettes. The roads here were laid out for holiday homes which, fortunately, were never built.

3 Sa Caleta

The urban development along this stretch of the coast (mainly villas) is discreetly hidden by tree cover. Beyond is the prettily named Cala Niu Blau (Blue Nest Cove), a 100m (110yd) stretch of sand with a café but little else.

4 Cala Pada

This attractive bay is a popular destination for families taking the ferry shuttle from Santa Eulària. There are a couple of beachside cafés here if you have built up an appetite, and you may even be tempted to go for a paddle in the shallow, transparent water.

5 Cala s'Argamassa

From Cala Pada, the path continues past the cluster of modern hotels that constitute the mini-resort of s'Argamassa. The path hugs the coast before turning inland to cross the rocky promontory of Punta Arabí, from where there are fine views of two islets, Isla Rodona and its larger neighbour, Isla de Santa Eulària.

6 Es Canar

The Club Punta Arabí dates from the early 1970s and spawned the famous Hippy Market, which you could visit if you happen to be here on a Wednesday (*see pp60–61*). Otherwise, stroll on to Es Canar, a busy but nevertheless beautiful cove with a Blue Flag beach and excellent watersports facilities. You can now either return to Santa Eulària on foot or hop on a ferry (summer only).

Pedalos are for hire at Cala Pada

Hippies

Disillusioned with capitalism, the rat race and the consumer society, the flower power generation of the 1960s dreamed of an alternative society based on peace, love and communal living, a spiritual world at one with nature. Some found it in the souks and kasbahs of Marrakech, others in the temples of Goa or the mountains of Nepal, still others found paradise in two small Mediterranean islands.

Getting into the beat at Benniràs

It all started in 1958 with the opening of Ibiza airport. First came the beatniks, then the hippies, a colourful collection of idealists and dreamers, mystics and gurus, rebels and dropouts, Beat poets and psychedelically inspired artists, peaceniks and draft dodgers fleeing the war in Vietnam. The hippies' hedonistic philosophy was light years away from the dour conservatism of the Franco era, but Ibiza was too remote and unimportant for the dictator to take much notice of this influx of foreigners. Its attractions in those days were even more obvious than now. Of course there was the sunshine, the beaches and the scenery, but back in the 1960s the roads were deserted, the coastline was undeveloped and one could get by on virtually nothing.

The first hippy haunts were the Can Tiruit commune at Sant Joan de Labritja in the northeast of Ibiza and the Fonda Pepe bar at Sant Ferran on Formentera. The folk singer Bob Dylan stayed here for a while before moving on to El Pilar de la Mola further to the east, where it is said that he lived in a windmill. Another popular

The Hippy Market at Es Canar

hangout was Anita's bar in Sant Carles, just down the road from the hippy market at Las Dalias. Naked revellers held impromptu love-ins on the beach at Es Cavallet or worshipped the setting sun at Benniràs. In 1973, the shrewd owners of Club Punta Arabí agreed to allow half a dozen stallholders to sell their wares on the patio, and the Es Canar Hippy Market was born.

It was a film by the French director Babet Schroeder which put the islands firmly on the hippy trail. *More*, shot on location in Formentera in 1969, was the story of an American drug addict (played by Mimsy Farmer) and her doomed love affair with a naïve German student (Bulle Ogier). The British rock band Pink Floyd supplied the soundtrack and the psychedelic tale achieved cult status, especially in France where it created a minor sensation. Ibiza was now officially hip and celebrities, such as Polish film director Roman Polanski and 1960s pin-up Ursula Andress, began buying holiday homes on the island.

The dream was destined not to last. In 1968, 41 hippies were deported after being found guilty of drug dealing and 'immoral conduct'. Few tears were shed by the native islanders who, amused and indulgent at first, had come to tire of their 'dirty' lifestyle and drug-induced antics. By the early 1980s, the tourist boom was pushing prices through the roof, while the commercialism the hippies so despised was now rampant. A few determined souls stayed on, but most left to pursue more conventional careers and lifestyles. But the hippy legacy can still be detected in the Ad Lib fashion movement, the New Age drumming rituals at Benniràs, the hedonistic excesses of the clubbers and the markets at Es Canar and Las Dalias. Without the hippies, Ibiza and Formentera would have been very different places.

From Cala Nova to Es Figueral

You'll have to walk or cycle a short way from Es Canar to reach the wild, desolate beach at Cala Nova. There's a campsite nearby, but few families venture down as the rocky shoreline is not well suited to children. It's possible to swim, but windsurfing is more popular here. Snacks are available from the *chiringuito* at the back of the beach in summertime. If you're here out of season, bring a picnic – the chances are you'll have the place to yourselves.

Just around the headland from Cala Nova is **Cala Llenya**. *Llenya* means 'wooded', and older residents remember a time when the area was a mass of pine trees. They're now confined to the back of the beach, a crescent of white sand, hemmed in by low cliffs. When the weather turns blustery the windsurfers arrive (boards are available for hire here). Three kilometres (2 miles) further on is **Cala Mastella**, one of the most delightful spots on this stretch of coast. The bay is formed from two coves which give the small beach of ochre sand an intimate feel. This is a great place for a swim, and if you've built up an appetite the temptation to linger over a seafood lunch at Joan Ferrer's restaurant, El Bigotes, may prove irresistible. Once rested, you could take the scenic coastal road from here to **Cala Boix**, a long narrow strip of dark, pebbly sand. To get down there you'll need to be fit, though – access is via a flight of stone steps carved out of the rock. Beyond the promontory of Cap Roig (Ibiza's most easterly point) is **Pou d'es Lleó**, a picturesque spot where the fishing huts are a reminder of older Ibizan traditions. 'The lion' is a reference to the Roman legion once stationed here, while 'pou' is the small spring which is the focus of a religious procession on 8 August. The clear waters and interesting rock formations attract snorkellers. Follow the steep path up from the beach to inspect the *atalaya* (watchtower). It was built to observe the island of Tagomago, once used as a base by Barbary pirates preparing to raid Santa Eulària. From Pou d'es Lleó you can drive on to **Es Figueral**, a small resort popular with families, with a beach nearly 300m (1,000ft) long. From here it's only a short hop to **Aigües Blanques**, the island's oldest nudist beach.

The beach at Cala Pada is popular in summer

Beyond Punta Arabí

On the other side of Es Canar, past the wooded headland of Punta Arabí, are more enticing coves and beaches, popular with families and day trippers from Santa Eulària. There are splendid vistas of the rocky islets of Rodona and Santa Eulària from **Ca na Martina.** Scuba diving expeditions set out from here to explore the red coral that thrives around the underwater caves. Equally busy and more developed than Ca na Martina, **Cala s'Argamassa** has a small sheltered beach, liable to be crowded in season. Watersports range from pedalos and banana boats to parasailing. The mini-resort of **Cala Pada** is only a 3km (2-mile) drive from Santa Eulària but the boat excursion (summer only) is a more relaxing alternative. The main attraction is the 200m (656ft) long sandy beach, where young children enjoy paddling in the shallows. There are several café-restaurants to choose from and excellent watersports facilities, including parasailing, diving and windsurfing. The local sailing school hires out catamarans.

One of the coves of Cala Mastella

Walks from Cala Llonga

It is possible to reconnoitre the cliffs on either side of the inlet at Cala Llonga. The first route, to a blowhole on the northern side, takes about an hour and a half and is a fairly easy climb along a tarmac road and a footpath. The second route up to the cliff top at the southern end of the bay is a bit more demanding, but worth the effort for the commanding views of the south of the island.

Allow 3 hours for both walks.

WALK 1

1 Bay views, Cala Llonga

Head north along Cala Llonga high street towards the edge of town, taking the side turning up the hill by the supermarket. Turn left at the top and continue up the hill, passing the El Dango apartment complex on your right. From the higher reaches there are superb views across Cala Llonga bay.

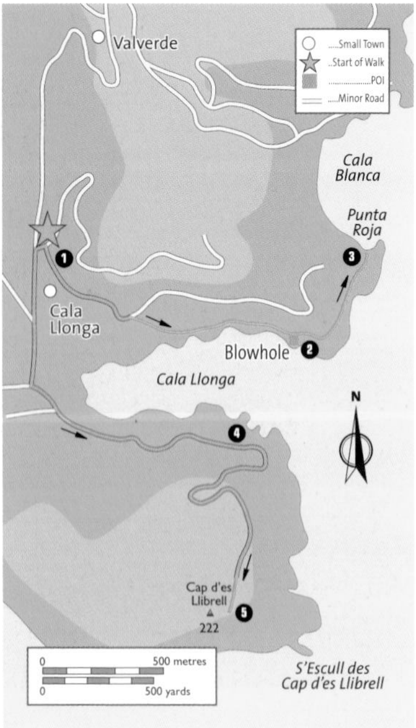

2 Blowhole

At the point where the road divides, take the right fork and continue as far as the roundabout. From here take the path heading off into the woods and up onto the cliff. As you emerge from the tree cover, you will see a small cave with a blowhole at the bottom. It's a bit of a scramble down, but worth the effort to watch the sea spray shoot up the vent under pressure from the waves below.

3 Punta Roja

Stroll on towards the end of the peninsula and you will be rewarded with views as far as the island of Formentera and along the coast to Santa Eulària.

WALK 2

4 Two views

Leave town on the road behind the Cala Llonga Hotel. Continue along the same route as the road becomes a track, threading its way up the thickly wooded hill and turning completely back on itself several times. The first *mirador* (viewpoint) overlooks Formentera and Santa Eulària Bay. The second is a stunning rearward look at the emerald waters of Cala Llonga. Unfortunately, you will find that the track peters out shortly beyond this point.

5 The lookout

Take the footpath directly in front of you, which bears slightly left as it enters the woods. It is narrow and overgrown in places, but the route is marked at regular intervals by piles of stones. Follow the path to the top of Cap d'es Llibrell. At 222m (728ft), this vantage point has been of great strategic importance. It was known to the Moors, and was regularly manned by sentries on the lookout for pirates. Its last visitors were Nationalist troops during the Civil War. The panorama is a full 360°, but keep well away from the cliff edge.

Safe haven – yachts enter the tranquil bay of Cala Llonga

Santa Eulària des Riu

Santa Eulària's compact new town (Sa Vila Nova) was laid out in the 1940s on a grid pattern, making it easy to find one's way around. Its detractors criticise it for being bland and short on atmosphere. Certainly life here is lived at a more sedate pace than in Sant Antoni or Eivissa (the almost total absence of nightclubs keeps the ravers at bay), but for many visitors this is a distinct advantage.

The focal point of the new town is the Passeig Marítim, a palm-fringed promenade with a decorative fountain, antique gas lamps and immaculately kept miniature gardens. A leisurely stroll will bring you to the Port Esportiu, the largest marina in the Pitiusas, with more than 750 berths. This is not the place to shop for bargains or dine out on the cheap, but it does boast the only nightclub in town. The local diving school is also based here and boat charter is available at a price. For most visitors, Santa Eulària's greatest asset is not the marina but the gently shelving town beach, a dazzling expanse of whitish sand directly below the promenade. Families, especially those with young children, decamp here in numbers, and spaces are at a premium by lunchtime. If you do intend spending time here, bring some head cover and plenty of high-protection sunblock as there are no beach umbrellas for hire.

Santa Eulària boasts the only proper river in the Balearics (hence 'des Riu'), but anglers won't find much to write home about as it is bone dry for most of the year. Situated at the river mouth, **Platja des Riu** is the closest alternative to the town beach. There are a couple of restaurants here and, if you're an early riser, you can watch the sunrise as the fishermen unload their catch (it is sometimes called the Mariners' Beach). For a pleasant pre-dinner stroll, follow the landscaped course of the river upstream as far as the old bridge (no more than a few hundred metres).

The most promising streets for restaurants in Santa Eulària are Carrer Sant Jaume (good for tapas) and the parallel Carrer Sant Vicent. Both issue out of Plaça d'Espanya, an attractive square where flowering oleander and hibiscus offer a dash of colour. The monument here pays tribute to the bravery of Santa Eulària's fishermen, who saved the shipwrecked crew of the *Mallorca* from drowning in 1913. The pedestrianised Passeig de s'Alamera is the focus of a mini hippy market every day except Wednesday and Sunday. Basket weaving, ceramics and other Ibizan handicrafts are showcased here and in the adjoining side streets. To describe Santa Eulària as a centre of culture would be gilding the lily, but it was the long-time home of a minor Impressionist painter, Laureano Barrau (*see p77*), and a number of artists have set up home here. Wander around the small local galleries or try to catch one of the exhibitions (details from the tourist office). If you are exploring the town with children in tow, one way to coax them into a bit of sightseeing is to hop on the Santa Eulària Express, a miniature train which leaves from the town hall and tours the Ibizan countryside before ending up at Puig d'en Missa, with a refreshment stop and opportunities to visit the church and museum.

Puig de Missa

Santa Eulària's disarmingly beautiful old quarter is ten to fifteen minutes' walk from the new town. It is difficult to believe nowadays, but until the 20th century this *was* Santa Eulària. It was the Romans who first bridged the river and stationed a garrison in the area, though they never built a settlement. Neither did the Arabs, who preferred farming the surrounding countryside, well irrigated in those days by the *riu.* Only after the Catalan conquest did local farmers begin building houses on the slopes of the hill, around a Christian chapel dedicated to Santa Eulària (first mentioned in 1305). This was razed to the ground by marauding pirates in 1555, stirring Felipe II of Spain into re-fortifying the settlement. The Berbers tested out the new defences in 1621 but were repulsed, and from then on the inhabitants were allowed to live in peace. The Puig de Missa that visitors see today has barely changed since the 18th century, when it comprised (apart from the church) five streets, a fountain and a flour mill.

Plaça d'Espanya from Passeig de s'Alamera

Taken together, it is an architectural gem, its stark simplicity to be savoured and contemplated.

Visitors first arrive at the portico or *porche* of the church, which was added in the 17th century. After the hill climb, it makes sense to rest for a few moments beneath the beamed roof, supported by gleaming whitewashed arches and massive pillars. The Italian military engineer Giovanni Battista Calvi is usually credited with the design of the church, little more than a nave and apse – the two side chapels, doubling as transepts, were added around the same time as the portico. The thickness of the outer walls means that temperature and humidity levels are constant throughout the year. Sad to relate, nearly all the interior decoration was destroyed in a fire during the Civil War. The present Spanish Baroque high altar comes from a church in Segovia, while the image of the patroness dates only from 1940. Stop by the cemetery to admire the magnificent views of the town and bay before taking a look at the bastion adjoining the church. This lookout tower has no inner rooms and was accessed via a ladder on the church roof, where cannon were placed.

Església de Puig de Missa (church). Open: Tue–Sat 9.30am–2pm. Free admission.

Historic Puig de Missa church with its domed roof

Don't leave Puig de Missa without visiting the **Museu d'Etnografia d'Eivissa** (Ethnographic Museum) on the Can Ros estate. The building is a typical, flat-roofed Ibizan house of the kind that fascinated architects Le Corbusier and Josep Sert. The exhibition space serves as the perfect introduction to a way of life that has now all but disappeared. Visitors enter via the *porxo* or hall (the main living space), before moving on to the kitchen, the wine cellar, the *trull*, where olive oil was produced, and the sleeping quarters. The rooms contain fascinating displays of jewellery, costumes and espadrilles, toys and musical instruments, fishermen's gear, agricultural and carpentry tools – there's even an original corsair's licence. You can see craft demonstrations (wickerwork, embroidery and so on) during the summer.

Museu d'Etnografia d'Eivissa. Open: summer Mon–Sat 10am–2pm & 5.30–8pm, Sun 11am–1.30pm; winter

The simple beauty of Puig de Missa church

Tue–Sat 10am–2pm, Sun 11am–1.30pm. Closed: mid-Dec–Jan Sun. Admission charge.

Sant Carles de Peralta

As there are only three bus services a day during the week to Sant Carles (although there are more at the weekends and in summer), it makes sense to drive or take a taxi the 7km (4 miles) from Santa Eulària, perhaps stopping along the way to buy some of the produce from the local farms and market gardens. Sant Carles itself is little more than a cluster of whitewashed houses and a church dating from the beginning of the 19th century. The building is usually locked, so you are unlikely to get much further than the porch, a double arcade of doughty columns supporting a pine-timbered roof. While you are cooling off here or maybe writing a postcard, spare a thought for the local curate, executed by the Republicans in the early months of the Civil War, when the church was ransacked and its furnishings destroyed.

Signs near the bus stop point the way to **Anita's Bar**, still trading profitably

A breathtaking view over Sant Carles de Peralta

on its 1960s hippy associations. The Ibizan liqueur, *herbes eivissenques*, and a range of appetising meals are served up on the covered terrace, a more attractive option than the rather gloomy dining room.

Take the Santa Eulària road from Sant Carles and on your right (ten minutes on foot) is **Las Dalias**. The hippy market here, while smaller than Es Canar (*see pp60–61*), has a more authentic feel – there is more than a whiff of cannabis about the place. Browse the stalls for handmade kaftans, beaded handbags, cashmere shawls, silk pyjamas, statuettes of Indian goddesses, African drums and the like. Plump up a cushion in the souk-like café and you could be heading down the road to Marrakech. Alternatively, call in at the pub restaurant and ask the locals about the hippies who made good – some bought *fincas* (farms) in the area.

As much more of a locals' market, Las Dalias is open all year, and during the December Christmas Market visitors are treated to hot snacks and glasses of mulled wine.

S'Argentera

The countryside around Sant Carles is remarkably unspoiled and so peaceful that you can drive for miles and not hear anything but birdsong. If you are tempted to linger, head for the *mirador* at S'Argentera, 110m (361ft) high, from where there are panoramic views across the coastline. S'Argentera means 'silver', a curious misnomer as it was lead that was mined on the hillside here from Roman times. Puig de S'Argentera is now a miniature nature park. Leave the car in the car park, pick up a map and follow any of the trails through the pine woods. You may stumble across some of the mine workings, which were not finally abandoned until the early years of the 20th century.

Es Trui de Can Andreu

Follow the road from Sant Carles to Cala Llenya and within a couple of minutes you will come to this well-preserved *casament* or farmhouse, now converted into a small but appealing museum. The name Es Trui refers to the enormous olive press on show in the kitchen, without a doubt the prize exhibit. The owner takes visitors on a guided tour of the house and there is a shop selling local wines.

Hand plough on display outside Es Trui de Can Andreu

Walk: Exploring Santa Eulària des Riu

This circular walk starts on the promenade in Santa Eulària and takes in the old settlement of Puig de Missa. The modern municipal capital dates only from the beginning of the 20th century and was laid out on a grid pattern in the 1940s. The focal point is the town hall on the leafy Plaça d'Espanya.

Allow 2 hours.

1 Riu de Santa Eulària

The only river in the Balearic region is hardly worthy of the name. In medieval times the *riu* flowed freely, irrigating what was then highly fertile land. Now, though 11km (7 miles) long, it is little more than a trickle for much of the year. However, the local council has landscaped the banks near the estuary, with gardens and a children's play area.

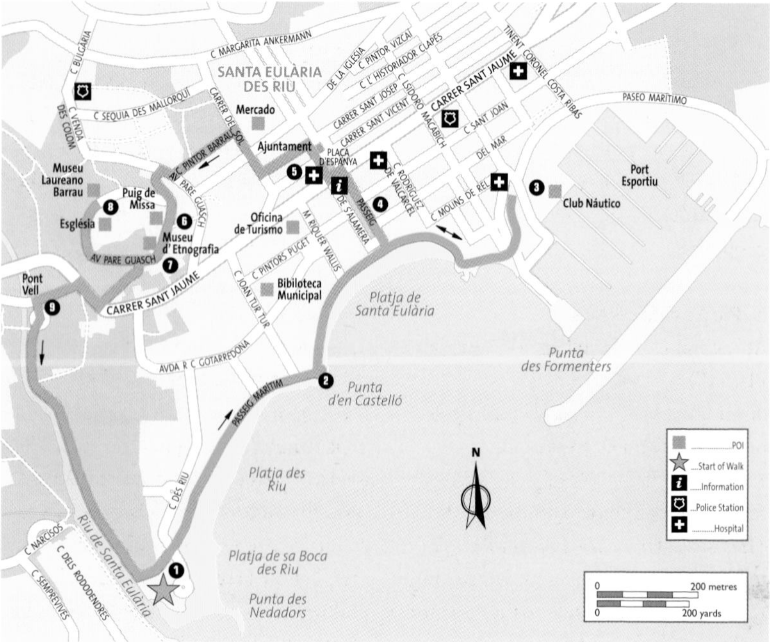

2 Passeig Marítim

Stroll along the palm-lined promenade past two arcs of fine, white sand – the Platja des Riu (River Beach) and the smaller (but busier) Platja de Santa Eulària. The sheltered waters of Santa Eulària bay are ideally suited to jet- and water-skiing – aficionados of both sports practise on the river beach.

3 Port Esportiu

The marina at the northern end of the promenade is the largest in the Pitiusas. The restaurants and shops are pricier than those inland, and unless you are feeling particularly flush you probably won't want to linger.

4 Passeig de s'Alamera

Return to the promenade and turn right onto the wide, leafy avenue known as Passeig de s'Alamera. This pedestrianised street is the heart of Santa Eulària's shopping area, and is good for souvenir hunting.

5 Plaça d'Espanya

At the top of Passeig de s'Alamera is Plaça d'Espanya, a small square dominated by the colonnaded façade of the Town Hall. On the corner of Sant Jaume is The Royalty, a café-restaurant dating back to the 1930s. They serve late breakfasts on the terrace as well as cakes and ice creams, so this is an ideal place to put your feet up for a few moments.

6 Puig de Missa

Turn left onto Carrer Sant Josep (behind the Town Hall), then right onto Carrer del Sol. When you reach the produce market bear left onto Carrer Pintor Barrau and start the steepish climb past picturesque whitewashed houses to Puig de Missa.

7 Two museums

There are two small museums on the hill. The more immediately appealing is the **Museu d'Etnogràfia** (Ethnographic Museum) on the Can Ros estate. Next to the church is the house of Laureano Barrau, a Catalan Impressionist who liked to paint the Ibizan countryside, especially the coastline around Santa Eulària.

8 Església (church)

At the top of the hill is the 16th-century fortress church complete with circular defence tower (*see pp71–3*). This beautiful church forms the nucleus of Puig de Missa, and from here there are panoramic views of the town and bay.

9 Pont Vell

Take the footpath which starts 50m (55yd) above the Ethnographic Museum and leads down to Carrer Sant Jaume. Turn right here, then, after another 50m (55yd) or so, bear left onto the path which leads to Pont Vell, a 17th-century bridge with three stone arches, now used only by pedestrians. Follow the footpath beside the river to return to Platja des Riu.

Serra de Els Amunts

The pine-carpeted massif of Els Amunts covers an area of around 100sq km (39sq miles) from Cap Nunó to Sant Vicent. The relatively heavy rainfall here makes it one of Ibiza's most fertile regions – wine, olives, almonds and lemons all thrive on the terraced hillsides. Approaching the coast, the scenery becomes more rugged and dramatic, the crags and stacks of the sheer cliffs inhabited only by cormorants, peregrine falcons and Audouin's gulls.

Since 1991, most of the coastline has been protected as an area of special natural interest and is perfect for hiking. The area also boasts some of Ibiza's most beautiful coves, many of which are sufficiently off the beaten track to deter the package tourists based in the built-up resorts of Sant Miquel, Portinatx and Sant Vicent.

Cala Benniràs

There are stunning views from the coastal road skirting this pearl among coves. Take care with the descent as the path is especially slippery after rain. One of Benniràs' attractions is the absence of hotel development. Another is the fine expanse of pebbly sand at the end of a long inlet, sheltered by pine-wooded hills. The rocks on either side of the bay make it a paradise for snorkellers. The amenities are more than adequate: showers, umbrellas, sun loungers, a *chiringuito* and a couple of restaurants. It was the mystical associations of Benniràs that attracted the hippies back in the 1960s. Fellow travellers still make the pilgrimage on August full moon, when they drum through the night for world peace.

Cala des Portixol

One of Ibiza's more isolated coves, Cala des Portixol is well worth tracking down. It can be reached by car with a walk to follow. (There is no *chiringuito*, so pack a picnic.) From Sant Miquel de Balansat, take the road west in the direction of San Mateo, turning off at signs to Isla Blanca. Just beyond the holiday homes is Manolo's bar (closed out of season). Leave the car here and follow the dirt track. After about 30 minutes you will be rewarded with wonderful coastal views towards **Cap Rubió** (Blond Point, 315m/1,033ft). Sea birds perch in niches in the fissured cliffs, and if you have binoculars you may catch a glimpse of the rare Eleanora's falcon. Tucked away in the small inlet down below is a pebbly beach with a cluster of

Cala Xarraca enjoys an idyllic setting

fishermen's huts, but little else. Arrive before lunch and you may even have the place to yourselves.

Cala Xarraca

Between the holiday resort of Portinatx and Sant Joan de Labritja lies Xarraca, an extensive bay with three excellent beaches. The rocky shores and transparent waters are an open invitation to snorkellers; bathers, however, should tread carefully on the seabed. **Cala Xarraca**, the busiest of the three, also has the most room – the mud baths to the west do wonders for skin tone. Next door is **S'Illot des Renclí**, named after a tiny offshore islet. You may see fishermen dragging their boats onto the shore here – some of the catch will be served up to patrons of the cliff-top restaurant. An inviting prospect is **Cala Xuclà**. It is without question one of the most beautiful spots on the island and is a mere stroll away from Cala Xarraca. The superb setting and remote location are an instant recommendation to anyone seeking peace and solitude, but come early in the season – Xuclà's charms are no longer a secret.

Cova de Can Marça

This 100,000-year-old cave system was formed by a river burrowing under the hillside. It is of interest to naturalists as well as geologists, since bone and fossil remains of long-extinct species have been found in the rock. In more recent times, smugglers used the caves to hide contraband liquor – they found an entrance below the present one and

Nature works its magic in the Can Marça cave

hauled themselves up with the aid of ropes and hoists. There are spectacular views as one makes the steep descent from the café terrace (and ticket office) to the entrance, approximately 12m (40ft) above the sea. (Vertigo sufferers may want to give this one a miss.) The guided tour – in English – lasts about 20 minutes and is rounded off by a set-piece sound and light show around an artificially created cascade suggesting the appearance of the chamber and galleries in the dim and distant past.

Port de Sant Miquel

The lovely pine-wooded approach to this busy resort, about 5km (3 miles) from Sant Miquel de Balansat, offers few hints about what lies in store. For more than 30 years, the view to one side of the bay has been marred by an ochre-coloured hotel with extensive terraces. Port de Sant Miquel caters more or less exclusively for German and British holidaymakers, especially families with young children. This is reflected in the menus of the resort's plentiful bars and restaurants. Sant Miquel's most obvious asset is its gently shelving, sandy beach, where there are excellent opportunities for watersports. There is no shade, though, and precious little elbow room by the end of June. If the crowds cast a pall, try your luck elsewhere. **Caló des Moltons**, to the west, has a *chiringuito* and beach umbrellas and is accessible on foot. Alternatively, you can drive to **Es Pas de S'Illa des Bosc**, which takes its name from a small offshore islet. Set back from the cliff is an 18th-century *atalaya* (watchtower), Torre de Mular.

Portinatx

Ibiza's most northerly resort has shed the last vestiges of Spanishness in the quest to lure ever more foreign visitors. During the season, day trippers on round-the-island tours disgorge onto the largest of the three beaches, **S'Arenal Gros**, from the coach park opposite. The shops and restaurants trailing up the hill offer the predictable tourist fare of burgers and pizzas, so if this prospect fails to entice, continue in the direction of **Cala d'en Serra**. Within ten minutes you will be enjoying the fragrance of the pines, still abundant in this part of the island. The 7km (4-mile) hike to the beach should take no more than an hour and a half – drivers will have to walk the last 200m (220yd). Snacks are available from the *chiringuito* and there are umbrellas and sun loungers for hire. Bring a pair of sandals and watch out for the rocks when swimming.

Cala d'en Serra, just ten minutes from Portinatx

A walk in the woods exploring the country park at Can Pere Mosson

Sant Joan de Labritja

A post office, a mini-market and a petrol pump – on the face of it, there's not much to detain the visitor in this village on the road from Eivissa to Portinatx. Yet there is more to Sant Joan than meets the eye, for example the paradox that a community of around 400 people should have its own town hall. In fact, Sant Joan is a municipality covering more than a third of the island. The parish church was completed around 1770, except for the belfry (*c.*1900), which purists have criticised for being out of keeping with the whole. Sant Joan was a focus for the hippy community in the late 1960s. One German visitor to the island at that time went on to found **ECO** (*www.eco-ibiza.com*), an Internet café with an attractive garden terrace, just across the road. ECO also runs an organic market and a New Age bazaar and organises everything from car hire to entertainment at children's parties.

Sant Llorenç de Balàfia

Stop long enough in the village to admire the stark geometrical minimalism of the church, then head off to the real point of local interest, about 1km (2/3 mile) to the east on the Eivissa to Portinatx road. Balàfia derives from an Arab word meaning 'health-giving fountains', a clue to the medieval origins of the place. As late as the 16th century, this was the *only* inland settlement of any importance on the island, a distinction that did not escape the notice of the North African corsairs. When they were sighted off the coast (usually in the dead of night), a patrol would set off cross-country to inform the inhabitants of this mini-citadel. The thick, interconnected walls of the half-dozen (still inhabited) houses are a reminder that they were as much a part of the defences as the sturdy ochre-coloured bastions – the lime crosses were to ward off evil spirits. As in Santa Eulària, would-be assailants were bamboozled by the absence of a door – access was via an upper-storey terrace on which a ladder was planted when the need arose. Take the Es Figueral road from Balàfia and you will pass Ca na Pepeta, a restored *granja* (farmhouse) serving excellent, reasonably priced regional cooking.

Can Pere Mosson Nature Park occupies the wooded hill above the church at Sant Llorenç (the entrance is next to the church). There are marked hiking trails and barbecue areas with pleasing views of the surrounding countryside.

A medieval tower stands guard over Balàfia

PUNTA DE SA CREU

This spectacular *mirador* offers one of the finest views on the north coast. To get there, follow the road north to San Miquel, then take the signposted turning to the Hotel Hacienda at Na Xamena (the first five-star hotel on the island). To the right, a rough surfaced road branches off in the direction of the coast. To the west of the headland is Portixol and Cap Rubió; to the east, beyond Port de Sant Miquel and the Can Marça caves, lies the magnificent cove at Benniràs. Not even the heliport can intrude on the beauty of the spot.

Sant Mateu d'Aubarca and around

The wild, remote stretch of coast from Cala d'Aubarca to Cap Nunó has, mercifully, escaped the attention of the developers, largely because of the stony beaches. Cala d'Aubarca is best reached on foot (from Sant Mateu, take the Camí d'Aubarca road at the church – if you are driving you will have to walk the last kilometre or so). In the Middle Ages falcons were bred here, and they still nest in the clefts of the rock. To the left, behind the headland at **Cap d'Aubarca**, are two ruined bastions and a section of broken wall, all that remains of the **Torres d'en Lluc**. The origin of these defences, which probably date from early medieval times, is shrouded in mystery. It has been suggested that they were intended to ward off attack from enemies on another part of the island rather than to guard the coast. The cliffs at Cap Negret are the tallest in Ibiza at 375m (1,230ft). To get to the *mirador* here, follow the Can Gorra path from Santa

Sant Mateu is an up-and-coming wine-growing region

Agnès. To the east, beyond Cala d'en Sardina, is **Punta de ses Torretes**, a tooth-like promontory with a cleft just wide enough for small boats to pass through. Offshore are a couple of tiny islets known as Ses Margalides, breeding ground of the Ibizan green lizard. A side turning 2km (1 1/4 miles) off the Santa Agnès–Sant Antoni road leads to the **Cova des Vi** (**Ses Fontanelles**). The cave paintings discovered here in 1917 were originally thought to date from the Bronze Age (2nd millennium BC). An alternative theory is that the depictions of boats (unfortunately badly weathered) are Punic, the authors possibly being watchmen guarding the lookout tower at Cap Nunó. The cave is closed to the public for the foreseeable future.

Sant Miquel de Balansat

By common consent, the parish church of this small village, built on a hill 175m (574ft) above sea level, is among the most beautiful on the island. Founded shortly after the Catalan invasion in the 13th century, it is also the oldest, although nothing of the original building survives. A gateway with a triple arcade leads to a spacious inner courtyard, like the thick walls, designed to ward off enemy attack. The overall harmony of the building is the more surprising given that the nave was not completed until the end of the 17th century. The wall frescoes date from the same period. Every Thursday evening from 6.15pm to 7.15pm (June to Sept), the Colla de Balansat dance troupe performs outside the church.

Sant Vicent de sa Cala and around

There are two scenic routes to the bay of Cala Sant Vicent, one following the pine-wooded road from Sant Joan, the other negotiating a tortuous corniche with breathtaking views of the bay and the island of Tagomago. Down below, sheltered by the hills, is the beach, a perfect arc of fine sand, 400m (1,312ft) long and 40m (131ft) wide. The setting is undeniably magnificent, though the hotels and holiday villas that have accumulated here over the years tend to detract from the natural beauty of the bay. Cala Sant Vicent has excellent watersports facilities (snorkelling, diving and water-skiing, for example), but essentially this is a family resort. During summer, boats leave on excursions to Tagomago and the beaches at Es Figueral and Pou d'es Lleó. The nudist beach at **Aigües Blanques** (popular with gay visitors) is also nearby. To get to the stony but virginal cove of **Port de ses Caletes**, at the foot of Puig de sa Fita (308m/1,010ft), you will have to take the signposted road from Sant Vicent de sa Cala – little better than a rough track in places – then walk. There is no beach to speak of nor anywhere to eat or drink, but the mirror-clear waters, sheltered by towering cliffs, are ideal for swimming and scuba diving. By far the best way to explore this area is on foot. Pick up a map from the tourist office and follow the blue signs along the Ruta des Falcó hiking trail to the hamlet of **Sant Vicent de sa Cala** (3km/2 miles inland) where there is little to detain you, apart from a typical Ibizan church, dedicated in this case to the medieval firebrand preacher, St Vicent Ferrer (patronal day, 5 April). There is another Ruta des Falcó from the village to **Punta Grossa**, the lofty promontory that shelters Sant Vicent beach. The views along the way are nothing short of spectacular. Just north

An art gallery in Santa Gertrudis de la Fruitera

The 303m (994ft) peak of Sa Talaiassa towers over Sant Vicent de sa Cala

of Cala Sant Vicent is the ancient Carthaginian sanctuary at **Cova des Cuieram.** (To get there, take the paved road from the east end of the bay to the car park, then follow the signs to the cave, a steep uphill climb.) The finds here have been dated to between the 5th and 2nd centuries BC. Copies of the terracotta statuettes dedicated to the fertility goddess Tanit are now on sale in almost every Ibizan gift shop, but to see the originals you will have to pay a visit to the Archaeological Museum in Eivissa (*see p41*). You will find that the views of the coastline are well worth the trouble.

DEATH ON THE BEACH

In 1936 the body of Raoul Villain was found on the beach at Cala Sant Vicent with a bullet through the throat. A right-wing nationalist, Villain assassinated the great French socialist Jean Jaurès. After being acquitted in 1919, thanks to the chauvinistic climate in France at the end of World War I, he bought a house in Ibiza and went into hiding. But the Spanish Republicans caught up with him during the Civil War. His whereabouts were betrayed and, after a summary interrogation, he was executed.

Santa Agnès de Corona and around

Between Sant Mateu and the pretty hamlet of Santa Agnès lies the fertile Vall de Corona, planted with olives, citrus trees, vines and almonds which flower in January and February scattering white and pink petals over the encircling hillsides. The young, but eminently palatable, wines produced here have long been valued by the locals and are now gaining recognition further afield (*see pp170–71*). There are no official tours, but the owners of the **Bodega Sa Cova**, about 1.5km (1 mile) west of Sant Mateu, are happy to show visitors around with advance warning. The village also hosts a wine festival in December. Five kilometres (3 miles) from Sant Mateu, Santa Agnès is a pleasant spot to stop for refreshment, though there is little to see apart from the tiny church (1806).

On the square, *bocadillos* (bread rolls) filled with cheese and mouthwatering *tortilla* (omelette) are the speciality of Can Cosmi, which has a terrace and a good selection of home-made dishes.

Bodega Sa Cova. Tel: 971 18 70 46.

Santa Gertrudis de la Fruitera

As its name suggests, fruit growing has long been the mainstay of this small agricultural community. In recent years well-heeled townies have been building second homes in the vicinity, which accounts for the boutiques and art galleries. If you are interested in antiques and bric-a-brac, check out the website of the English auction house, **Casi Todo** ('almost everything'), for information about the monthly sale (*see p147*). Terrace bars and restaurants cluster around the main square, by the typical fortified church (1796).

Casi Todo. www.casitodo.com

Disarming simplicity – the dazzling façade of Sant Vicent's minimalist church

Walks from Santa Agnès

There are two scenic cliff-top walks from the attractive village of Santa Agnès de Corona. The first heads towards the rugged cliffs of the north coast, before doubling back to Sant Mateu d'Aubarca. Allow 4 hours to cover the 15km (9 miles). A less demanding alternative is to follow the circular route around the picturesque Corona plateau (about 8km/5 miles – allow 2 hours). Take some water with you, as there are few shops or cafés en route.

PATH TO THE NORTH COAST

1 Vall de Corona

Leaving Santa Agnès by the small lane at the side of the church, you will soon begin to cross the magnificent Corona valley, one of the most fertile parts of the island, thanks to the rich reddish soil and sheltered aspect. All kinds of crops grow here, from vines and cereals to lemons, figs and almonds.

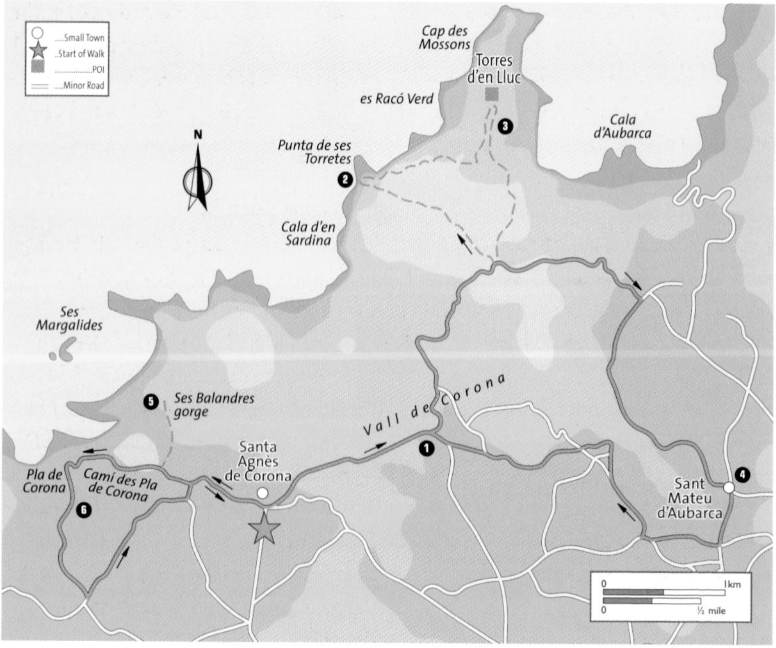

2 Cala d'en Sardina

When you see a fork in the road after about 1.5km (1 mile), turn left towards the coast. Continue through the wood, which becomes denser as you make your way up the hill at the side of the valley. After another kilometre (2/3 mile) take the footpath branching off to the left, which leads to the cliffs above Cala d'en Sardina. Straight ahead is the rocky promontory of Punta de ses Torretes with coastal views to either side.

The vineyards at Sant Mateu

3 Torres d'en Lluc

Follow the line of the cliffs towards Cap des Mossons, and at the beginning of the headland you will see the remains of the mysterious Torres d'en Lluc. No one knows why or when these towers were erected, although it has been suggested that they were part of a fort protecting a coastal settlement (which no longer exists) from possible attack from inland. Stretching below is the majestic bay of Cala d'Aubarca.

4 Sant Mateu d'Aubarca

Take the path from Cap des Mossons and descend through thick woodland to the Vall de Corona, then take the left fork to Sant Mateu d'Aubarca. Call in at the village bar to sample the *vi pagès* (local) wine, before returning along the track through the valley back to Santa Agnès.

THE CORONA PLATEAU

5 Ses Balandres gorge

From the centre of Santa Agnès take the Camí des Pla de Corona. Where the road bends to the left, turn right onto the farm track. Continue through the wood and the rough track becomes a footpath. After about 1km (2/3 mile) you'll reach the Ses Balandres gorge. It's a tough, slippery descent to the sea below; it would be better to walk to the *mirador* to the west of the gorge. From the cliffs here you can look out to the crescent-shaped island of Ses Margalides.

6 Pla de Corona

Take the footpath back through the trees and return to the Camí des Pla de Corona. Turn right. When the road turns off to the left, continue along the path, keeping to the edge of the fields. The Pla de Corona, a plateau ringed by gently undulating hills, is 200m (656ft) above sea level. The rich palette of colours in the patchwork of fields makes for a good photograph. Follow the path inland as it rejoins the dirt track, and at the next junction turn left, back across the fields to Santa Agnès.

Ancient sites

Over millennia the Pitiusas were visited by successive waves of invaders and colonisers – Bronze Age farmers, Phoenician and Carthaginian traders, Roman and Byzantine artisans and craftsmen. A number of sites have already been uncovered, although archaeological knowledge of the islands' history and prehistory remains sketchy. The pick of the finds is exhibited in the Archaeological Museum in Eivissa (*see p41*), and while there is not always that much to see *in situ*, the settings are usually worth a visit in themselves. The museum at the Puig des Molins necropolis (*see pp55–6*) is closed for renovation until further notice. For information about its reopening call 971 301 771.

Ca na Costa

When the megalithic monument at Ca na Costa on Formentera was discovered in 1974, it aroused great excitement among archaeologists as it established beyond doubt that the Pitiusas had been settled long before the Phoenicians arrived in the 7th century BC – more than 1,000 years earlier, in fact. The funeral chamber, a circle of jagged stones, was approached via a rectangular atrium and narrow corridor (originally covered). Apart from the expected axe heads and bone tools, the remains of eight individuals – six men and two women – were unearthed at the site.

Cap de Barbària

See p124.

Cova des Cuieram

Several pieces of evidence attest to the religious significance of this small cave. First, a Punic inscription was discovered in the 1920s: 'For

The ancient stone circle at Ca na Costa

Finds from historic sites are exhibited in Eivissa's Archaeological Museum

Abdesmun son of the priest Azarba'al, for our lady Tanit, the powerful.' Secondly, there was evidence of a small altar with a scattering of animal bones suggesting sacrifice. Finally, hundreds of terracotta statuettes of the Carthaginian fertility goddess were found in the recesses of the chamber. *1km (2/3 mile) north of Cala Sant Vicent – follow the signed footpath. Open only with official guide.*

Cova de ses Fontanelles

See p99.

Sa Caleta

Excavations at Sa Caleta, the first Phoenician settlement in the Pitiusas, were completed in the early 1990s and covered an area of some 4ha (10 acres). The colonists, several hundred all told, are thought to have arrived from southern Spain in around 650 BC. Visitors can see the foundations of a number of buildings, including houses (originally of more than one storey), storerooms and iron-smelting workshops for making tools and weapons. After barely half a century, the Phoenician settlers decided to move the capital to Eivissa, and Sa Caleta was abandoned for good. When they left, they took everything of value with them, even cleaning up before they went. *Between Es Condolar and Cala Jondal. The site is open to the public but is surrounded by a metal fence.*

Ses Païses de Cala d'Hort

For well over a millennium (450 BC to AD 700) the hillside overlooking Es Vedrà was inhabited by Punic, Roman and Byzantine communities who earned a living from farming and fishing. Finds from the largest of the buildings here, dating from the 1st century AD, suggest that it was put to agricultural or commercial use with storerooms, wine cellars and kitchens built around a large central courtyard. Nearby are the remains of two necropolises, one from the Carthaginian era, the other Byzantine. *About 2km (1 1/4 miles) from Cala d'Hort, off the Cala Vedella road.*

Sant Antoni de Portmany and the west

Ibiza's largest town after Eivissa boasts a magnificent harbour and a nightlife second to none. But if clubbing is not the reason you came to the island, use the port as a base for exploring the west coast. Catch a boat to one of the three Blue Flag beaches in the area or head north to the coves. A boat excursion to the rocky islet of Es Vedrà is the ideal curtain raiser for the Cala d'Hort Nature Reserve.

Some history

The cave paintings at Ses Fontanelles point to a human presence in the area during the Bronze Age. The Romans valued the harbour, calling it Portus Magnus ('large' or 'great' port), but it was not until after the Catalan invasion that Sant Antoni was settled by colonists from the mainland under the command of the Count of Roussillon. They farmed the area behind the port, growing wheat, barley and other crops. The fields were irrigated by the Torrent de Buscastell, a stream that flowed into the harbour. In 1305 the Archbishop of Tarragona authorised the building of a chapel dedicated to Saint Anthony, patron saint of animals and agriculture. This was replaced by a fortified church after Sant Antoni was sacked and destroyed by Berber pirates in 1383. The defences were refined over the centuries – there were cannon on the roof until 1869.

The modern history of Sant Antoni begins in the 1960s with the arrival of the first wave of tourists in what was then the proverbial sleepy fishing village. The developers went to work with a vengeance, and by the 1980s Sant Antoni had grown into a mega-resort with an unenviable reputation for heavy drinking, drug taking and loutish behaviour, with most of the blame laid at the door (with good reason) of the British contingent. The authorities were forced to step in, since when things have quietened down, though the West End

'*UC*'

Visitors to Sant Antoni may notice a statue by local sculptor António Hormigo on Carrer Ramon y Cajal. Completed in 1977, its official title is *Es Verro* (The Brave One), but everyone refers to it as 'The Shouting Man' because of the hands cupped in front of the mouth. Actually, the subject of the sculpture is making the '*uc*', a strange guttural sound unique to the Pitiusas and thought to originate in pre-Roman times. Some suppose it to have been a war cry, others a primitive form of communication. *Ucadors* are proud of their abilities and can produce subtle variations in rhythm, pitch and tone.

still has a somewhat sleazy reputation. 'San An' belongs to the clubbing fraternity in July and August, but families are beginning to return here at other times of the year.

The promenade

The palm-fringed promenade (Passeig de Ses Fonts, Passeig de la Mar) was one of the improvements introduced during the 1990s to offset the town's downmarket image. Beyond the Yacht Club, which offers sailing lessons, and the several-hundred berth marina is the Moll Vell, the old dock where fishermen still land their catches. Passeig de Ses Fonts comes into its own on Sant Antoni's two red-letter days, 17 January and 24 August, when the celebrations include a huge firework display. However, you can catch something of the festive flavour on Sundays from November to April, when the local folk troupe performs the *ball-pagès*, a traditional dance unique to the Pitiusas (*see pp19–20*).

The Egg sculpture, Sant Antoni

Call at the tourist office by The Egg (*see box below*) for information about local walks: there are four *Rutas des Falcó* of between 2 and 10 kilometres (1¼ and 6 miles) exploring the environs of Sant Antoni, and a more demanding 23km (14-mile) hike to Santa Agnès de la Corona, reaching deeper into the surrounding countryside. These walks are signposted in five different colours.

MONUMENT TO THE DISCOVERERS

Known irreverently as The Egg, the symbolism of this odd-looking monument derives from an apocryphal anecdote concerning the explorer Christopher Columbus. Looking for a sponsor to back one of his expeditions, and being told that it was impossible, the great man picked up an egg and asked whether anyone could stand it upright. After much shoulder-shrugging on the part of his audience, Columbus achieved just that by cracking and removing part of the base. 'Nothing is impossible' was his comment, and the rest, as they say, is history.

Walk: Platjes des Comte

Only half an hour's bus ride to the southwest of Sant Antoni is the scenic coastline of the Platjes des Comte, an area of natural beauty that is protected by law. This walk takes in some of the best bays and coves and is far from strenuous. There are plenty of opportunities to buy drinks along the route; however, some kind of headgear is essential as there is little shade from the sun.

Allow 2 hours to cover the 6km (4 miles).

1 Platjes des Comte

Buses leave from Sant Antoni to Cala Bassa for the Platjes des Comte, the starting point of the walk (there are two buses in the morning and two in the afternoon). The beaches of Cala Conta and Cala Comte are among the most beautiful on the island, though sand is at a premium along this rocky shoreline. The sea is crystal clear, however, and the views of the coastline and the small islands offshore are really splendid.

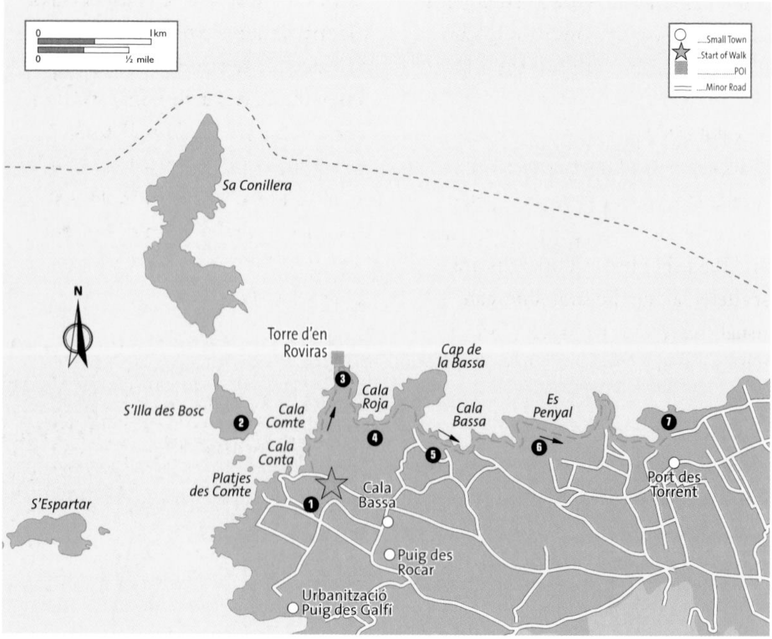

2 Three islands

Start walking from the beaches in a northerly direction across the sandstone cliffs and look out at three islands which form part of the Cala d'Hort Nature Reserve. The nearest, and smallest, is S'Illa des Bosc. The name means 'wooded isle', although this hardly fits the bill today. To the south lies the long, straggling island of S'Espartar, while to the north, rising like a humpback whale from the sea, is Sa Conillera.

3 Torre d'en Roviras

Follow the edge of the cliff, keeping an eye out for the indigenous green lizard, which makes its home in the dry scrubland. Continue to the Torre d'en Roviras, an 18th-century watchtower. From here there are even better views of Sa Conillera and, in the opposite direction, the bay of Sant Antoni.

4 Cala Roja

Walk on beyond the tower in the direction of Sant Antoni and you'll pass Cala Roja. There is no beach here and the fishermen, whose huts are scattered along the shoreline, can usually carry on with their work without being disturbed by visitors.

5 Cala Bassa

Cross the headland at Cap de la Bassa and descend to the cove of the same name (Cala Bassa). The locals reckon this is the finest beach on the island, and the European Union agrees, awarding it Blue Flag status – you may be tempted to stop here for a swim. If you decide to stay longer, there are several cafés to choose from, and in summer boats depart from here for Sant Antoni.

6 Es Penyal

Beyond Cala Bassa the path ascends again to the cliffs at Es Penyal, where you might see the storm petrel or the Balearic shearwater; both nest on the offshore islands between March and June.

7 Port des Torrent

Next stop is the busy resort of Port des Torrent, nowadays little more than an extended suburb of Sant Antoni. Torrent refers to a stream that flows down here from Sa Talaiassa, Ibiza's highest peak, before emptying out into the bay. The beach is popular with day trippers and you may find the crowds off-putting, although the terrace of the Can Pujol restaurant makes a pleasant lunch stop. Conceivably you could walk back to Sant Antoni from here, but there isn't much in the way of scenery. It makes more sense to take the bus from the holiday village, or the ferry shuttle (summer only).

Cala Comte

Sant Antoni

For a quick dip, the town beach at S'Arenal or the string of rocky coves further around the bay will suffice. However, the water quality here is not all that it might be – better to explore the more inviting beaches, less than half an hour's journey away by boat or bus. Scuba diving and other watersports are available at various points along the promenade. For other sporting options, *see pp160–61*.

Sa Cova de Santa Agnès

Hidden inside the mouth of a small cave, 1.5km (1 mile) north of town on the Santa Agnès road, is an ancient shrine, thought to date from around the 4th century AD. Interestingly, pottery fragments and other remains from the Punic era have been found, suggesting that this Christian place of worship, one of the oldest on the island, may originally have been a pagan sanctuary. About 100m (328ft) away is a 16th-century chapel, now the Sa Capella restaurant, which serves traditional Ibizan cuisine.

Església de Sant Antoni

Although its origins are much older, the present parish church dates mainly from the 17th century, when the splendid polygonal tower was added as a defensive measure. There are two other noteworthy features, the portico to the side of the church and the *azulejos* (painted tiles) which decorate the base of the interior walls. Only the statue of Saint Anthony survives from a 17th-century retable that was destroyed in a fire during the Civil War.

The 17th-century Església de Sant Antoni

Taking in the glorious sunshine along Cala Moí

Punta des Molí

The rocky promontory at the far end of S'Arenal beach (overlooking Platja des Pouet) takes its name from a flour mill, which has been restored and is open to visitors. You can see the hydraulic machinery for pumping water, the *trull* where olive oil was produced, and a typical village house, used for temporary exhibitions.

Sunset Strip

This is the popular name for the parade of upmarket bars and nightclubs on the way to the beach at Caló des Moro. The 'old timer' here, Café del Mar, was founded in 1980 and is still going strong. Since 1994 the house DJs have been producing their own chill-out CDs at the rate of one a year. Sipping a cocktail on the terrace of Mamba, Savannah or Coastline as the sun sets is a relaxing way to pass the early evening.

West End

English is the *lingua franca* of this part of town where every other building is a pub selling the great British breakfast, cut-price beer and live sport on TV. After dark the street sellers appear, hawking the predictable range of watches, junk jewellery and sunglasses to would-be customers on their way to one of the noisy clubs, the other speciality of the West End.

One of Ibiza's best-kept secrets, the sheltered cove of Cala Gracioneta

Cala Gració

Sadly, the ravages of the developers have taken their toll on Cala Gració's beautiful setting, while the shimmering expanse of fine, white sand attracts too many visitors at the height of the season, when the pleasure boats drop anchor here on their way from the Cap Blanc aquarium. Better to take the path by the fishing huts on the north side of the bay to the neighbouring inlet of **Cala Gracioneta**. The beach here is no more than 30m (100ft) wide, but this is a beautifully sheltered spot, perfect for swimming and with a *chiringuito* serving meals almost at the water's edge. Surprisingly, Gracioneta's existence passes almost unnoticed.

To drive to Cala Gració from Sant Antoni takes a matter of minutes and is hardly worth the effort. A healthier alternative is to cycle or walk, taking the detour suggested by the Ruta des Falcó, to the palaeochristian chapel at Sa Cova de Santa Agnès. (Leave Sant Antoni on the Santa Agnès road: *see p104.*) A little further on from Cala Gració is the *mirador* **Cap Negret**, from where there are stunning views of the island of Sa Conillera. Nudist sunbathing is common on the rocky promontory of Punta de sa Galera, between Cap Negret and Cala Salada (follow the footpath from Sa Cova de Santa Agnès).

Cala Salada

This magnificent cove at the end of a pine-forested road is only 5km (3 miles) north of Sant Antoni. The beach is off to the right – take the path by the stone tower. Sun worshippers may be happy to bask on the rocks near the boathouses, though it is difficult to see how anyone can resist a dip in the clear turquoise waters. Cala Salada's surroundings are surprisingly unspoilt, given its proximity to Sant Antoni, but, for the same reason, it is unlikely to be deserted. The locals, who need no reminding of its charms, moor their boats here at weekends. It may be difficult to land a table at the fish restaurant, built on a series of terraces near the cliff. Do try, though – the fish stew speciality, *caldereta de langosta*, is mouthwatering. If you are still feeling adventurous, you could take the footpath leading directly from the cove to Puig Nunó, passing Cova de ses Fontanelles on the way. It is tough going in places but worth the effort for the wonderful coastal views.

Cova de ses Fontanelles

The Cave of Springs is also known as the Cova des Vi because wine was once stored here. The paintings on the walls of the chamber are thought to depict boats, although they have been weathered by erosion and are now only faintly discernible. They were discovered in 1917 by the French archaeologist Henri Breuil, who dated them to the Bronze Age. More recently, scholars have suggested that they are Punic, pointing out that the Carthaginians built a watchtower on nearby Cap Nunó.

Half a kilometre (1/3 mile) inland from Cala Salada (follow the signs). The paintings are protected by a grille and can be seen from the outside.

Tranquil Cala Salada, less than 15 minutes' drive from the bustle of Sant Antoni

Beaches to the west of Sant Antoni

Four kilometres ($2^1/_2$ miles) from Sant Antoni, at the western edge of the bay, Port des Torrent is an extension of the town and heavily developed on all sides, except to the rear of the beach, where the pines have been left undisturbed. There are umbrellas and sun loungers for hire, and a choice of places to eat and drink, but not much else to recommend the resort. Give this one a miss and head for the twin beaches of Platjes des Comte. Both **Cala Conta** (the larger of the two) and **Cala Comte** enjoy the coveted Blue Flag status, with small stretches of golden sand – no shade, though – and superb snorkelling and diving conditions. Urban development has been kept at bay and there are fine coastal walks through pine-scented scenery (*see p94*). There are bus and ferry services to Cala Conta during the summer, but despite the ease of access relatively few day trippers get beyond Port des Torrent.

Closer to Port des Torrent and equally well served by local transport is **Cala Bassa**, just around the headland of Punta de sa Pedrera. The gently shelving beach and sandy seabed (also Blue Flag) are the big draw for families with young children – pedaloes and banana-boat rides are also available.

Sa Conillera Archipelago

From Cala Comte one can clearly make out three islands, of which **Sa Conillera** – 'Rabbit Island' – is the largest (*see pp94–5*). Sadly, the story that this was the birthplace of the Carthaginian general, Hannibal, has been all but discounted. Equally fanciful, but more entertaining, is the folklore that witches collect the grasses needed for their secret potions here on St John's Eve (23 June). Barbary pirates used Conillera as a base to attack Sant Antoni, which explains the presence of the watchtower on Punta de sa Torre. The 19th-century lighthouse has a range of 30km (19 miles) and warns sailors of the treacherous reefs

Splashing around at Cala Conta

A yacht anchored at Cala Bassa

lurking in the strait between Sa Conillera and its nearest neighbour, **S'Illa des Bosc**. Once densely wooded (hence the name), this was the proverbial port in a storm for stranded fishermen, though it looks pretty inhospitable at a casual glance. It was once inhabited by charcoal burners, which explains why the forest is now denuded. The former residents of **S'Espartar**, the third island in the group, augmented their diet with seagulls' eggs and *virot* chicks (a kind of shearwater).

The Conillera archipelago is part of the Cala d'Hort Nature Reserve (*see pp107, 110*) and an important conservation area. The crevices in the limestone rocks are a breeding ground of the endangered Balearic shearwater (*Puffinus mauretanicus*), which was here long before man came on the scene – fossil remains have been found from the Pleistocene period. Serious ornithologists organise boat trips to the more remote archipelago of **Ses Bledes**, around 3km (2 miles) further out to sea. A graveyard of merchant shipping from Punic times onwards, Ses Bledes was fomerly used by whalers.

Clubbing

Ask anyone under 40 to name one thing they associate with Ibiza, and the chances are it will be clubbing. Every year from June to late September the island's dance meccas rock to the Ibiza Sound, a catch-all phrase for a bewildering variety of musical styles, spawned by the synthesiser but with little else in common apart from a pounding drum underlay. For many years, dance music was a largely British phenomenon, but Spanish, Italian and German interest quickly grew, thanks to the commercial success of a handful of party anthems. Dedicated aficionados save up for months to be able to enjoy the full clubbing experience. They come for the music, the company, the spectacle, the drugs in some cases, but above all they are here to have a good time – 'larging it', to borrow from the vernacular.

The Eden nightclub is a paradise for today's Adam and Eve

The Ibiza scene has its origins in the hippy counterculture of the 1960s, which offered an alternative lifestyle to the repressive Franco dictatorship. The first club, Amnesia, was little more than an overgrown disco operating from a converted farmhouse on the road to San Rafel. The action soon moved out of doors and, as more clubs began to appear, the rave was born. At the same time, the influence of the home-grown Balearic Beat – a mixture of electronic, Latin and Afro funk sounds – on British Acid House in the mid-1980s gave birth to dance music and the clubbing phenomenon. When the island authorities banned open-air partying at the beginning of the 1990s, the clubs responded by taking the action indoors, where it became more raunchy and outrageous with each successive season. Rock stars, supermodels and other A-list celebrities began dropping in, and the resultant publicity generated by the gossip columnists was a godsend for the promoters. Nowadays, you are more likely to see soap stars and game-show hosts, but, while numbers have been down of late, there is little evidence to suggest that the clubbing bubble is about to burst. Although there are some glimmers that Ibiza is returning to its hippy roots, the greatest threat to local dance culture may stem from the cavalier attitude of some club owners to noise pollution and other regulations.

Party till the morning after at Amnesia

A night out

No one is in the dark for long about where the action is. Fliers are distributed on beaches and in bars, while the major events are advertised on hoardings at the side of main roads. When deciding what to wear, the rule is: the more outlandish the garb, the better. In the world of clubbing anything goes, from basques to cami-knickers, from top hats to platform soles. Think 'fancy dress', and you can't go far wrong. Clubbers get into the swing in the 'warm-up' bars around the Passeig Marítim in Eivissa or the Sunset Strip in Sant Antoni. Some clubs have their own bars, and also their own restaurants. A particularly good one is the restaurant at Privilege in Sant Antoni. To avoid drinking and driving there is an efficient and cheap night bus service connecting the main clubs. *www.discobus.es*

GAY IBIZA

Ibiza, Eivissa especially, is now firmly established as a leading holiday destination for gay men, and there are plenty of gay-friendly hotels and *pensions* to choose from. For nightlife in Dalt Vila, head for the La Muralla bar, the Anfora nightclub or one of the many gay haunts on Sa Carrossa. The leather bars and boutiques on Carrer Mare de Déu (Sa Penya) are popular gay hangouts, as well as the outrageous Dôme bar near the fish market on Carrer Alfons XII, where transvestites and drag queens like to strut their stuff on the terrace. Gay men congregate on the nudist beaches of Es Cavallet, especially around the Chiringay beach bar – open summer only – and at Aigües Blanques on the east coast. Most of the mainstream dance clubs advertise gay nights – look out for the promotional literature. For more information, visit *www.gayinspain.com* or *www.universogay.com/ibiza*

Drives from Sant Antoni de Portmany

The first of two possible routes explores the unspoilt villages of the island's hilly northern interior with stunning views of the countryside along the way. The round trip is about 50km (31 miles). Allow 4 hours.

The alternative route takes in some of the best beaches of the Cala d'Hort Nature Reserve. Distance: 30km (19 miles). Allow 3 hours.

PART ONE

1 Santa Gertrudis de Fruitera

Leave Sant Antoni on the C-731 to Sant Rafel – not much to see here apart from the ceramic workshops along the way – then take the scenic Santa Eulària road, passing the Hipódromo (racecourse). Turn left at the next junction (5km/3 miles) and head for the lovely little village of Santa

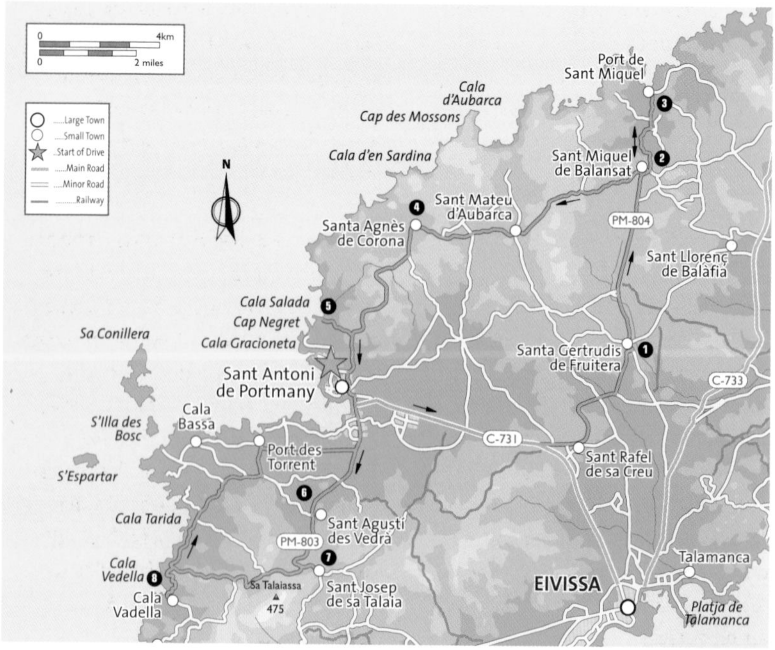

Gertrudis de Fruitera, possibly stopping for a delicious *jamón serrano* (cured ham) *bocadillo* on the terrace of Bar Costa.

2 Sant Miquel de Balansat

From Santa Gertrudis it is only a short drive to the village of Sant Miquel de Balansat. Leave the car for a quick look at one of Ibiza's typical fortress churches, perched high above the village on Puig d'en Missa. From the square outside there is a panoramic view of the thickly wooded hills of Els Amunts.

3 Port de Sant Miquel

A scenic but twisting 5km (3-mile) diversion from Sant Miquel brings you to the cliffs overlooking the sheltered bay of Port de Sant Miquel and the Can Marça cave beyond. After visiting the cave, you could have a swim in the resort.

4 Santa Agnès de Corona

The delightful side road from Sant Miquel to Santa Agnès de Corona passes Sant Mateu d'Aubarca, one of the smallest villages on the island, before winding through the Valle de Corona, a fertile plain, where the surrounding hillsides are planted with oranges, almonds and vines – wine growing is a speciality of the area. Santa Agnès is also famous for its fantastic *tortillas* (Spanish omelettes) – the Can Cosmi restaurant is a good place to sample them.

5 Cala Salada

Heading south from Santa Agnès, take the road to the right, a scenic, humpbacked route which threads its way back to Sant Antoni. Along the descent you will enjoy spectacular views of Cala Salada.

PART TWO

6 Sant Agustí des Vedrà

From Sant Antoni drive south in the direction of Sant Josep, looking out after 5km (3 miles) for the signs to Sant Agustí des Vedrà. Time seems to have passed by this tiny hilltop village, which is well worth a detour.

7 Sant Josep de sa Talaia

This small, well-heeled town is the centre of the municipality. Its shops, boutiques and restaurants are laid out around a modern square with plenty of shade. There are cash points here too, if funds are running low.

8 Cala Vedella and Cala Tarida

Take the same road out of town, but as you leave the houses behind, take the left fork heading towards the coast. This road offers good views of the pine-covered hillside of Sa Talaiassa, Ibiza's highest point. At the next junction carry on towards the coastal road to the beautiful coves of Cala Vedella and Cala Tarida, both good for swimming. From Cala Tarida it is a 10km (6-mile) drive back to Sant Antoni.

Sant Josep and the south

Sant Josep de sa Talaia takes its name from Ibiza's highest peak, Sa Talaiassa, from where there are commanding views of the island. The other main attraction of the region is its magnificent coastline, great swathes of which are safeguarded against future urban development. The Cala d'Hort Nature Reserve extends from just north of Cala Carbó to the rugged cliffs of Es Cubells. The Ses Salines National Park centres on the salt marshes, which gave birth to Ibiza's oldest industry.

Sant Josep de sa Talaia

To take the pulse of this thoroughly modern village – give or take an 18th-century parish church and a 1,000-year-old olive tree – find a table on the shady terrace of Can Bernat Vinya, the pick of the bars on the main square.

Sant Josep de sa Talaia's three-storey church is one of the most imposing in Ibiza

The locals drop in after Sunday mass for a few hands of *manilla* (a popular Spanish card game), oblivious, it would seem, to the creeping gentrification of their village. Next door is a shop specialising in embroidery, and you will also find a furniture shop where the owner likes to show visitors his interesting collection of folk instruments. Sant Josep's parish church was built by the villagers themselves as a labour of love. Work began in 1726 but was interrupted by an outbreak of plague. Four years later the Valencian architect Pere Ferrer was brought in to finish the job – the gallery running above the side chapels is a typical Valencian touch. Of the original Baroque retable, only the wooden figure of St Joseph was saved when the church was gutted during the Civil War. The current altarpiece, a replica, was installed in the 1950s. The *Colla de Sant Josep*, one of the best dance troupes on the island, performs outside the church on 17 July and 15 August at 9pm.

Cala Carbó

'Carbó' means 'coal' and harks back to the days when the impoverished inhabitants of Sa Conillera brought charcoal for sale in the small port. Since then, the pine woods behind the bay have been decimated to make way for building development, but the serene setting still seduces. You will need to get here early, though, as the pebble-and-sand beach is only 50m (55yd) long and fills up quickly. Stay long enough at any rate for a spot of lunch at the Restaurant Balneario. If the *guisat de peix* (a succulent stew made from a selection of fish and cooked with potatoes) is one of the specials, so much the better.

Cala d'Hort Nature Reserve

Inaugurated in 2002, this protected area extends over 3,000ha (7,413 acres), embracing the islands of the Sa Conillera and Ses Bledes archipelagos (*see pp100–101*), Es Vedrà (*see pp108–9*), the coastline from Cala Carbó to Es Cubells (*see pp110–11*) and the wooded slopes of Sa Talaiassa (*see pp114–15*). According to local ecologist José Ribas, up to 900 plant species need to be conserved, not to mention the

(*Cont. on p110*)

CELEBRITY HOMES

The Swiss film star Ursula Andress, star of the James Bond movie *Dr No*, was the first celebrity to buy a house in Ibiza – she lives in Es Cubells. Hard on her heels came the film director Roman Polanski, and there are now more than a dozen famous names with property here, including the three-times Formula One motor-racing champion Niki Lauda, 'mother of punk' Nina Hagen, the models Linda Evangelista and Jade Jagger, the rock star Noel Gallagher and Johnny Lee Miller of *Trainspotting* fame.

Cala d'Hort Nature Reserve

Boat trip: To Es Vedrà

Of the boat trips from Sant Antoni, the pick of the bunch is the cruise to Es Vedrà, a nature reserve and one of the island's truly awe-inspiring sights – bring a camera and binoculars. The excursion by glass-bottomed catamaran departs at 3pm every afternoon (summer only) and takes 3 hours. Tickets are available from kiosks on the waterfront an hour before sailing. Demand is high so do not wait until the last minute. The cruise includes a swimming stop.

Cala Tarida

The boat rounds the promontory at Punta de s'Embarcador, passing three or four inconspicuous inlets en route to the larger bay of Cala Tarida. The broken line of white buildings – small hotels and self-catering apartments for the most part – is all there is in the way of urban development. The rocky end of the beach is good for snorkelling, and scuba diving is also a possibility. The C'as Mila restaurant serves freshly caught fish from a terrace overlooking the bay.

Cala Molí

This small but enchanting cove, almost closed off by sheer cliffs and sheltered by pines and conifers which trail down to the beach of pebbly sand, is relatively quiet most of the time. The hilly countryside of the Serra de Cala Molí is good hiking territory.

Cala Vedella

This low-key resort caters mainly for families with young children – the calm waters and gently sloping beach of soft white sand are its obvious assets. Luxury yachts and motor launches anchor off the coast in the late afternoon – the sunsets are special here. There is a walk from Cala Vedella to Ibiza's highest peak, Sa Talaiassa, 476m (1,562ft) – ask at the tourist office for the relevant *Ruta de Falcó* map.

Cala Carbó and Cala d'Hort

(*See pp107 and 110.*)

Es Vedrà

The boat makes a complete circuit of this limestone colossus, its near-vertiginous cliffs towering 382m (1,253ft) above the sea and the smaller islet of Es Vedranell. Myth and magic are Es Vedrà's stock in trade. They say that this is all that remains of the lost continent of Atlantis and that Homer's hero Odysseus avoided shipwreck after being lured here by the Sirens. For centuries, Es Vedrà was uninhabited except for goats and rabbits. Then, in the mid-19th century, a Carmelite monk, Francesc Palau, came to live here as a hermit and reported seeing 'unearthly beings surrounded by light' – UFOs in modern parlance. More recently, Es Vedrà appeared as the fictional island of Bali Hai in the film version of *South Pacific* and on the cover of Mike Oldfield's album *Voyager*. As the boat rounds the island, train your binoculars on the cliffs for possible sightings of Audouin's gulls, shearwaters, shags, storm petrels and, if you are lucky, Eleanora's falcon. Few boats land here, none at all during the breeding season from 1 March to 30 September.

Cala Tarida is one of Ibiza's most appealing resorts

fauna and marine life. The natural beauty of Cala d'Hort makes it a location of choice for films and fashion shoots – its fans include celebrities like Goldie Hawn, Jade Jagger, Elle MacPherson and Mariah Carey. However, conservation activists are at loggerheads with Sant Josep council over the future of the luxury properties around Es Cubells, including villas owned by Spanish and foreign celebrities.

The views of Es Vedrà from the shoreline of **Cala d'Hort beach** are best enjoyed over a sundowner on one of the bar terraces. This lovely cove is a major draw at the height of the summer, but at other times of the year there is a good chance you will have the place to yourself. The offshore waters have near-perfect visibility to a depth of up to 8m (26ft), ideal conditions for snorkelling and scuba-diving. There are opportunities to see the *Posidonia oceanica* sea grasses, ammonites, cephalopods and other marine life, and fish such as wrasses, groupers, sea bream, mullets, rays and octopuses. Big Blue Dive, in Cala Vadella, also organises diving expeditions in the vicinity of Es Vedrà (*www.bigbluedive.net*).

Es Cubells

The cliffs above Cala d'Es Cubells seem an unlikely location for a church, but in 1855 the local fishermen, tired of tramping all the way to Sant Josep for Mass, persuaded their firebrand preacher to build them a chapel closer to home. Father Palau, a Carmelite monk better known for his lonely sojourn on Es Vedrà, consecrated the

The pebble beach at Cala d'Es Cubells

Off the beaten track – the charming village of Sant Agustí

oratory of Mare de Déu de Carme in 1864. From the road there are awe-inspiring views of the coastline from Cap Negret to Cap Llentrisca and of Formentera beyond. Dotted about the beach are the *chamizos* (thatched huts) where the local fishermen keep their boats. In days gone by this was a doubly dangerous occupation because of the constant threat of pirate attack. This was serious enough in the Middle Ages to deter the people of Sant Antoni from taking up fishing at all.

Sant Agustí des Vedrà

Bar Berri, Can Berri, and even the formidable-looking parish church, belong to the Berri family. At least it was one of their ancestors who paid for it – on condition, it is said, that the building was realigned so that he could see it from his house. Completed in 1806, the buttresses and side tower are clues to its defensive role; likewise the site, the highest point in the village, with commanding views across the west of the island. Everything in this one-horse town clusters around the Plaça Major, including Can Berri Vell, the oldest *finca* in Ibiza, now a restaurant serving mouthwatering pâté.

Ses Salines beaches

There are two fabulous beaches on the fringes of the salt pans, catering for anyone who enjoys music, beach bars, watersports and beautiful surroundings, but not necessarily peace and quiet. The nudist beach at **Es Cavallet** has been unofficially adopted by the gay community, while around the headland of Punta de sa Torre is Platja Migjorn, an equally dazzling stretch of white sand, bordered by dunes and pine trees,

The pristine sands at Ses Salines with typical conifer backdrop

universally known as **Ses Salines**. The actor Michael Douglas is one of a number of celebrities who occasionally drop in at Ses Salines' Sa Trinxa restaurant.

At the western end of the beach, near the bus stop, is **La Canal**, the small jetty where cargo vessels load up with salt, while a path to the rear leads to **Torre de ses Portes**, a watchtower once armed with three cannon and finally abandoned in the 19th century. From here there are wonderful views of the islets off the coast of Formentera, including Illa d'es Penjats (Isle of the Hanged), where executions once took place. Mounds of salt, waiting for collection from the pans, are clearly visible at **Es Condolar**, a beach littered with small stones, hence the name (from *còdol*, a dialect word for boulder). The best views of the pans can be had by walking the 5km (3 miles) from Ses Salines, across the back of Es Falcó 144m (472ft) to Es Condolar. The beach's setting would be idyllic were it not for the proximity of the airport. At the far end is the tiny cove of **Sa Caleta**. You could combine a swim here (*chiringuitos*, but no shade) with a spot of culture by visiting the ruined Phoenician settlement of the same name (*see p91*). Continue along the coast to **Cala Jondal**, whose sweeping stretch of pure white sand attracts families and young people. Clubbers gravitate towards Tropicana (chill-out music), while the beautiful people prefer Blue Marlin (rated among cognoscenti as one of the best beach bars on the island). The shoreline is stony, so if you intend to swim, flip-flops are a good idea.

Ses Salines National Park

The 400ha (988 acres) of wetland between Es Condolar and Ses Portes includes not just the salt pans (*see pp118–19*) but a natural environment with a unique cultural landscape: dunes and beaches, forests of juniper and sabine pines, defence towers, salt warehouses, windmills, waterwheels, wells and churches. The National Park is an ecosystem under special international protection and centred on the salt pans, a resource that has been exploited for more than 2,600 years. The roads, trails and pathways crossing the area are well signposted, and, as much of the terrain is flat, this is perfect cycling territory. A good place to start a tour is the old salt workers' chapel at Sant Francesc d'Estany, dating from the 18th century.

The adjoining cemetery had to be abandoned when it was discovered that the mineral-enriched soil was actually preserving the corpses rather than decomposing them. Take the footpath from the chapel to the Torre de Sal Rossa, one of two bastions constructed by the engineer Giovanni Battista Calvi in the 16th century to guard the salt works from pirate attack. Sal Rossa, literally 'red salt', refers to the pinkish tinge the granular crust acquires after evaporation. Its other name, Torre del Cargador, is a reminder of the longshoremen who loaded the salt here before the building of a new jetty at La Canal.

Salt pans, Ses Salines

Rock spiral at 'Atlantis'

What you see

The Ses Salines wetlands are an important habitat for nesting water birds and migrators sojourning here on their way to and from Africa. The Kentish plover, the black-winged stilt, herons, storks, flamingoes, terns, bitterns, grebes, ospreys, fisher eagles and egrets are among the 205 species that have been recorded in the course of a year. The salt pans are also rich in marshland and ocean-bed plants, molluscs, crustaceans and endemic insect species.

Practicalities

The tourist offices in Formentera (at the port) and in Eivissa town have information leaflets about the park, including maps with suggested walking and cycling routes graded according to difficulty. The most demanding of them covers the 19km (12 miles) from Platja d'en Bossa to Sa Caleta, taking in the beaches at Es Condolar, Es Cavallet and Ses Salines. Although the terrain is flat, only the fit should attempt the entire route in one day. When walking along the road, keep to the left so you can be seen by oncoming traffic. Bring some kind of head covering and sunblock in summer, wear strong, waterproof shoes and never leave without mosquito repellent. If you think you might be out after sunset, take a torch for walking in the dark. Cameras and binoculars are another must.

Sa Talaiassa

It was the Moors who gave Ibiza's highest peak its name (meaning 'watchtower'), and the panoramic views from the pine-carpeted summit explain why. You should have no problem making out the Bay of Sant Antoni, the salt pans of Ses Salines, the beaches of Es Condolar and Cala Jondal and the islet of Es Vedrà. On the clearest of days you may even be able to spot Mallorca and the outline of the Spanish coast. Sa Talaiassa is popular with ornithologists, who have recorded sightings of hoopoes, golden oriole and woodchat shrikes on the lower slopes, and crossbills and firecrests higher up. The rare Marmora's warbler has also been known to make an appearance. It is possible to drive to the summit, but if you are reasonably fit it is more rewarding to take on the 12km ($7^1/_2$-mile) hike from Sant Josep (*see p106*).

Torre d'Es Savinar

For some unforgettable views, follow the turnoff about 1km ($^2/_3$ mile) from Cala d'Hort, then take the signed turning to the *mirador* at Cap des Jueus and the watchtower of Torre d'Es Savinar, also known as the Pirate's Tower since 1909, when it featured in a novel by Valencian writer Vicente Blasco Ibáñez. They say that on a clear day you can make out the Spanish coastline from here. At the base of the cliff is Sa Pedrera, a quarry excavated in the 16th century to build the fortifications of Dalt Vila (*see pp34–7*). More recently, the hippies adopted the place for its karma, renaming it 'Atlantis'. Some are said to have experienced visions of the Buddha here, which inspired one artist to paint his image in a cave.

Es Vedrà from the 18th-century defence tower Torre d'Es Savinar

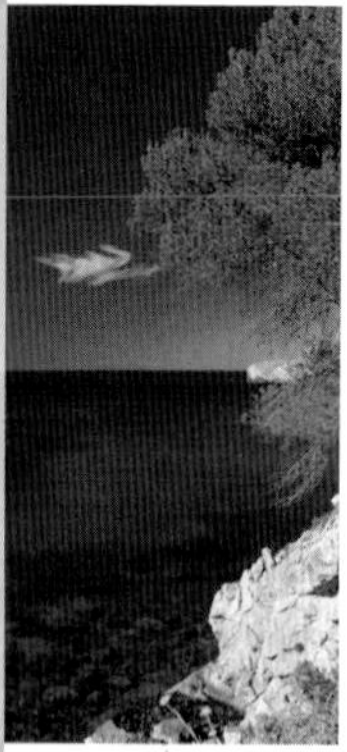

Walk: Sa Talaiassa and around

Nestling prettily in the valley below Sa Talaiassa, Ibiza's highest peak, Sant Josep makes a good base for hill walking. You can call it a day after climbing the peak if you wish, but if you still have reserves of energy and a couple of hours to spare, head for the beautiful coastline around Cala d'Hort. The going is not particularly tough, but you will need to set out early to avoid the full heat of the sun.

Allow 2 hours for the 6km (4-mile) hike to the summit.

1 Farmland

Leave Sant Josep on the Sant Antoni road. After about 2km ($1^1/4$ miles), turn left onto the signposted Sa Talaiassa track, a pleasant trek through walled citrus orchards and olive groves. On the way you will pass the Capella de S'Accident, a small chapel that commemorates the victims of an air crash that occurred here in 1972. Cheats drive to the top, so keep an eye out for cars en route.

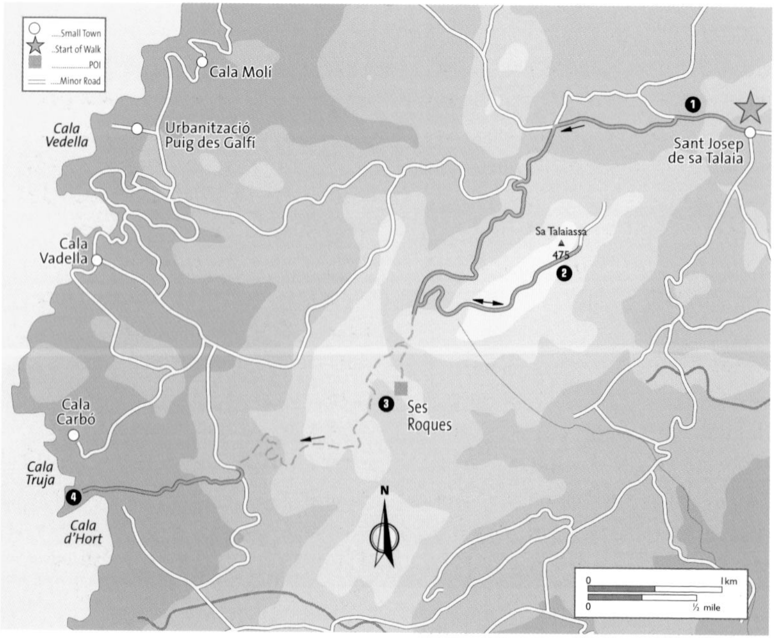

A stunning sunset over Cala d'Hort

2 Sa Talaiassa

As you approach the summit, the scenery becomes more rugged. Only the toughest plants seem to thrive in the rocky soil. The area around the radio mast has too much tree cover for views, but there are plenty of gaps a little lower down. On an exceptionally clear day, you might be able to make out Mallorca to the north and the Valencian coast of mainland Spain to the west. At the very least, you can see Ibiza spread out below you, and Formentera beyond.

3 Ses Roques

You can either return to Sant Josep at this point or retrace your steps back down the hill as far as the fork to Ses Roques, bearing left and then taking the path to Ses Roques, which you will see on the left, off the path to Cala d'Hort. This forested path leads to another vantage point, overlooking Cala d'Hort and the Es Vedrà rock. If you are here between April and November, look out for fleeting appearances of Eleanora's falcon, a rare bird that is indigenous to the Balearics.

4 Cala d'Hort

From Ses Roques retrace your steps in the direction of Sa Talaiassa, looking out on the left for the signposted path which will lead you on a steady descent towards Cala d'Hort. To get to the beach itself you will have to turn left onto the Cala Vadella road, then turn right. By the time you reach this legendary beach, famous for its transparent water, its sunsets and its views out to Es Vedrà, you will have earned a swim. You will also have built up an appetite; fortunately, there are several *chiringuitos* to choose from. The pick of the bunch is Es Boldado, but you may have to book ahead to get a table here.

Salt pans

When the Ses Salines National Park was created in 1995 it marked the end of a war of attrition between environmentalists and property developers that had been going on for a quarter of a century. Both the European Union and UNESCO have since recognised Ses Salines as worthy of special protection.

Origins

It was the Phoenicians who first saw the possibility of extracting salt from the coastal lagoons on either side of the Els Freus channel between Ibiza and Formentera. The export of 'white gold', used mainly for preserving meat (especially on board ship), proved to be so lucrative that the Romans and Moors had no hesitation in following suit. After the Catalan invasion in the 13th century, Jaume I allowed the islanders to exploit the salt pans themselves, and from then on profits from the sale were, in theory at least, divided equally. Extracting the salt was back-breaking work, carried out during the hottest time of the year (July and August) following the harvest. The crust on the surface was

Ses Salines beach

Salt has been a precious commodity since Phoenician times

broken and the salt cut into blocks, before being transported by mule for shipment from Sal Rossa (later from La Canal). Thousands died from malaria, carried by the mosquitoes that bred in the marshes, while murderous raids by marauding Berber pirates were a constant hazard. To protect the island's priceless industrial asset, Felipe II of Spain ordered the building of watchtowers at Sal Rossa and Ses Portes, using money from salt exports. At first workers from all over the island were drafted for the salt harvest, but over time a small community of labourers built homes near the pans and, in 1771, Carlos III of Spain allowed them to build their own church, Sant Francesc d'Estany (St Francis of the Salt Pans).

Today

Essentially the industry has changed little over the centuries. Tractors have replaced mules, and cargo vessels have taken the place of sailing boats, but the system of sluice gates, pumps and water channels that visitors see today is based on the technology introduced by the Moors in the 11th century. The harvest has fallen in recent years from a high point of around 80,000 tons (81,280 tonnes) to an average of 65,000 tons (66,040 tonnes). Most of the salt is exported to the countries of northern Europe, mainly for use in industry, but also for table salt. In Scotland it is used mainly for gritting roads in winter, while the Norwegians and Icelanders use salt for preserving cod.

Walk: Ses Salines National Park

A walk or cycle ride is the best introduction to the delights of this area. This route is about 12km ($7\frac{1}{2}$ miles) long, but you can break it up into smaller sections. Buses return to Eivissa from La Canal, Platja d'en Bossa and Sant Jordi. In the summer you will need a hat and some water, though you can buy food and drink along the way. Bring mosquito repellent in the summer, especially in September.

Allow 4 hours.

1 Sant Jordi

The church looks more like a fortress with its thick, windowless walls and crenellated battlements. In fact, like most of Ibiza's churches, it *was* a fortress, built to protect the local population from pirate attacks.

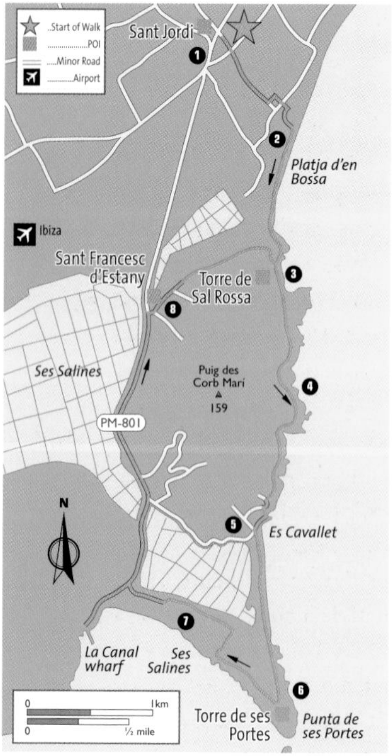

2 Platja d'en Bossa

The road opposite the church leads from Sant Jordi to Platja d'en Bossa. With 3km (2 miles) of fine, white sand, this is one of the island's more popular beaches, though it's more familiar to clubbers for the dance venue Space.

3 Torre de Sal Rossa

Head south to the quieter end of the beach where the path crosses an acrid water channel, carrying sea water into the salt marshes. The 16th-century tower was built to guard both Eivissa and the salt pans. From below, there are splendid views of Figueretes and the walled town of Dalt Vila.

4 Cliff-top stroll

The path skirts Cala de Sal Rossa (Red Salt Cove), then ascends to the cliffs. For the next 4km ($2\frac{1}{2}$ miles) you

Platja d'en Bossa is popular with clubbers

will be following the shoreline southwards, passing through pine forest and patches of sweet-scented rosemary. At the end you emerge onto Es Cavallet beach by the La Escollera restaurant.

5 Es Cavallet

Ibiza's first designated nudist beach is a vast expanse of pure, dazzling sand, backed by dunes and pines. If you can, avoid the temptation to linger and continue walking to Punta de ses Portes, the end of the narrow, rocky peninsula that marks the southernmost point of the island.

6 A chain of islands

From the defence tower here (Torre de ses Portes) you get a good view of the lighthouses on the islands of d'es Penjats and des Porcs. Beyond are the two closest islands to Formentera, Espalmador and Espardell. Cormorants sun themselves on the rocks around the point and you may even see the comparatively rare Audouin's gull – look for the red beak.

7 Ses Salines

Follow the path for about ten minutes, passing a series of miniature coves, and you will come to another superb dune beach known as Ses Salines. At the far end is the La Canal wharf, where salt is loaded for export.

8 Sant Francesc d'Estany

Pick up the main PM-801 road, which crosses the glistening pans, before skirting a hill called Puig des Corb Marí. Ahead of you is the church of Sant Francesc d'Estany, a chapel built in the 18th century for the salt workers. Just before you get to the church, you'll see a dirt track off to the right. Follow this back to the Torre de Sal Rossa and Platja d'en Bossa.

Formentera

Lying 16km (10 miles) south of Eivissa, Formentera is the smallest of the Balearic Islands, with an area of 84sq km (32sq miles) and a permanent population of nearly 6,000. Most of the terrain is flat, with the exception of the Cap de Barbària plateau in the south and the pine-forested hills of La Mola to the east, the highest point being Sa Talaiassa (202m/663ft). Nowadays, Formentera's residents earn their livelihood from tourism.

Most visitors to Formentera are day trippers, but an increasing number are tempted to spend more time here because of the beauty of the countryside – still largely unspoilt – and the fabulous beaches. To protect the environment, visitors are asked to explore the island on foot or by bicycle, though there is a bus service connecting the main villages and resorts. The tourist office in La Savina has brochures with suggested walking and cycling routes. This is also the place to ask about guided tours of Formentera's salt marshes, part of the Ses Salines National Park. Swimming, water-skiing, windsurfing, canoeing on the Estany des Peix lagoon, fishing and birdwatching are among the other activities available.

View north to Ibiza from Formentera

Some history

People were living on Formentera more than 4,000 years ago, and evidence of their activities has been discovered at three prehistoric sites, Cap de Barbària, Can na Costa and Sa Cala. The Romans farmed the land so successfully that they called it Frumentaria (Island of Wheat). They established a port in the natural harbour of Es Caló de Sant Agustí and built a military encampment to guard the approaches. After the Romans departed, the island was invaded by the Vandals, the Byzantines, the Arabs and the Normans, though there is no evidence that any of them settled here for any length of time. The situation changed after the Catalan conquest. Like Ibiza, Formentera was divided into *quartons* for administrative purposes and recolonised. Within a century, however, pirate raids and the ravages of the Black Death put paid to these plans, and the few islanders who remained were left to fend for themselves. It was not until 1697 that Carlos II of Spain entrusted the sea captain Marc Ferrer with the task of supervising the resettlement of the island, which took off surprisingly quickly after Formentera's defences were strengthened with a ring of new watchtowers. So successful was the repopulation that by the middle of the 19th century the island was unable to sustain the growing number of inhabitants, many of whom emigrated to Central and South America. Formentera's economy was saved by the timely arrival of the tourist boom in the 1970s, heralded by the hippies.

BIRDWATCHING

The Cap de Barbària is a great location for birdwatching. It is the first stop on the route from North Africa for migrating species such as the spotted flycatcher, woodchat shrike and nightingale, and a breeding site for the blue rock thrush, Thekla lark and red-legged partridge that nest among the rocks and rosemary bushes. Swooping around the headland itself are Balearic shearwaters, Audouin's gulls and peregrine falcons.

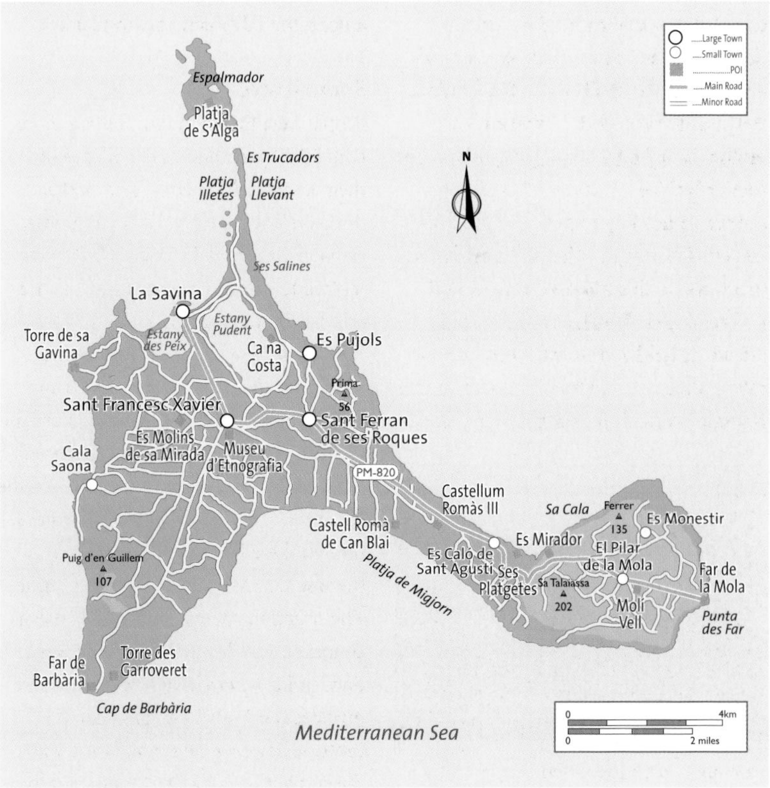

Barbària Peninsula

As one contemplates the increasingly arid landscape along the road south from Sant Francesc Xavier, it seems difficult to imagine this as the site chosen by the island's first settlers. Yet the evidence suggests a sizeable Neolithic community, making a living from raising livestock and rudimentary crop growing. There is no natural water source on the island, so the settlers must have collected rainwater in wells, as their descendants continued to do through the centuries, until the building of a desalination plant in recent times. The construction methods they used are similar to those of the Talayotic peoples of Mallorca and Menorca, suggesting possible trading links. Three sites have been excavated. Barbària II and III would have been living quarters, stables and workshops, while Barbària I is thought to have been a place of worship. All three sites are just off the main road and easy to locate. The name Barbària recalls the Barbary Coast of North Africa (little more than 100km (62 miles) to the south) and the pirates who were the bane of the islanders' lives for centuries. The 18th-century watchtower known as the **Torre des Garroveret** (to the left of the main road, just beyond the Neolithic settlement) is a reminder of those troubled times. Overlooking the cliffs at the cape, almost 80m (263ft) above sea level, is the **Barbària Lighthouse** (**Far de Barbària**) – next stop Algeria!

Ca na Costa

See p90.

Land's end at Cap de Barbària

Castell Romà de Can Blai

A turn-off near the 10km (6-mile) marker on the road from Sant Francesc Xavier leads to the remains of a Roman fort (*castellum*), thought to date from the 3rd century AD. One can make out the foundations of the perimeter wall and the bases of five rectangular towers, though little else. The encampment at Can Blai guarded the Camí Romà, then the most important road on the island, and the approaches to the port of Es Caló de Sant Agustí.

Es Caló de Sant Agustí

The northern coast of Formentera is much rockier than the south – windier, too. Nevertheless, there are some attractive spots here, among them Es Caló. The monks from the Augustinian monastery in La Mola used to moor their boats here in the 13th century, hence the name. The tiny cove, no more than 30m (100ft) wide, has been a port since Roman times and is still used by fishermen, although wood, coal and sandstone are no longer shipped to Eivissa and the Spanish mainland as they were in the 1920s. The beach is rocky and better suited to snorkelling than swimming, but the fish restaurants, with terraces overlooking the bay, are worth a look. Otherwise, track back along the coast to the beach at **Ses Platgetes** – much sandier and three times as wide. Alternatively, take the track (Camí Romà) from Es Caló up the hill to **Es Mirador** 1km (2/3 mile), from where there are wonderful panoramic views.

Espalmador

Espalmador is the largest of the islands off the coast of Formentera, privately owned but open to the public. The main attraction is the beach at **Platja de S'Alga**, popular with nudists (though not exclusively). The shallow waters are ideal for swimming and you can improve your skin tone by wallowing in the nearby mud baths. To escape the crowds in July and August, head around the coast to a pair of rocky coves known as **Cala de Bocs**. For centuries, Espalmador was populated exclusively by goats, but the island's strategic location put it in the front line of defence against the pirates – there was a permanent garrison here of around 50 soldiers. You can still visit the defence tower at **Sa Guadiola**, though you will not be able to see inside. There are excursions to Espalmador from La Savina during the summer.

Es Pujols

Four kilometres (2 1/2 miles) southeast of La Savina, Es Pujols is the island's main resort, founded at the beginning of the tourist boom in the 1970s but saved from unsightly overdevelopment when buildings of more than four storeys were outlawed. Behind the pristine beach of white sand is Avenida Miramar, a small promenade lined with fairly low-key bars and restaurants, serving everything from pizzas to fresh fish. There is more of the same on the high street, Passeig des Palmeres.
Es Pujols is also handy for shops, with

Fishing boat at Es Caló de Sant Agustí

The flat roads around Estany Pudent are good for cycling

a mini-supermarket or two, and several ATMs. The hinterland of Es Pujols is a wine-growing area, and you can see the vineyards if you take the *Camí de ses Vinyes* Green Route out of the resort towards Sant Ferran.

Estany des Peix

This shallow saltwater lagoon is connected to the sea by a narrow strait through which only very small craft can pass. Because it is closer to the sea than Estany Pudent (*see right*) it attracts gulls, terns and other seabirds. While the salinity level is not particularly high, it is enough for rushes, glasswort and other marsh plants of the *salicornia* genus to thrive. Centuries ago there was a small fishing port here, hence the name 'peix'. Near the road are the remnants of a prisoner-of-war camp where Republican soldiers were held following the end of the Civil War. A signposted Green Route skirts the perimeter of the lagoon, with panoramic views across La Savina towards the Es Freus strait.

Estany Pudent

This brackish lagoon only lives up to its name (meaning 'stagnant') on hot summer days when the sea is at low tide. The fetid conditions, produced by decomposing algae, are exacerbated by accumulations of rainwater, attracting swarms of mosquitoes. Salt concentration is high, three times that of the sea in places, although, surprisingly, some freshwater plants grow here, as well as the more predictable *salcornias* – rushes, giant reeds and sea violets. Flocks of several thousand black-crested grebe have been seen wintering on Estany Pudent, while the reed beds at the southern end of the lagoon attract little ringed and Kentish

(*Cont. on p130*)

Cycle ride: The northwest

The best way to get around Formentera is to cycle. The terrain is mostly flat, the climate mild and the views stunning, while the island is crisscrossed by unpaved tracks. This route explores the northwestern reaches of Formentera. It begins at the small resort of Es Pujols. It is about 28km (17 miles) round Estany Pudent and a further 16km (10 miles) to Cala Saona and back.

Allow 3 hours.

1 Ca na Costa

Take the Ses Salines road north from Es Pujols, passing a track on your left that leads to the stone circle at Ca na Costa. Here also are the remains of a megalithic burial ground, the most spectacular one in the Balearic Islands. The 2m (7ft) high slabs, discovered in 1974 and dating back to the early Bronze Age, are an important archaeological find as they were erected by Formentera's earliest settlers.

2 Ses Salines

Continue to Ses Salines and enjoy the natural beauty of Formentera's salt pans. These have been a conservation area since the salt works closed down in 1984.

3 Es Trucadors peninsula

Take the right fork at the pans and follow the track which leads to the tapering peninsula of Es Trucadors. After passing the windmill at Es Molí de Sal (now a restaurant), the path continues through a delightful dune-and-pine landscape revealing the stunning back-to-back beaches of Platja Llevant and Platja Illetes – a tempting point to dismount for a cooling swim.

4 Estany Pudent

Leave the peninsula by the same path, but before reaching the main road take the unpaved track to the right. This route, with the sea on one side and the lagoon on the other, was once followed by the industrial train transporting salt to the dock at La Savina. As the track enters the port, turn left to rejoin the road. After about 500m (1/3 mile), take the next left, which skirts the brackish saltwater lake of Estany Pudent. This is a nature reserve and a popular spot for birdwatching – look out for herons, egrets and possibly even a flamingo or two. Swimming is prohibited here.

5 Sant Francesc Xavier

At the southern point of the lake, follow the signs to the right and you will join the main road. Turn right again for Sant Francesc Xavier, the island's tiny capital. Take a short break in the sleepy village square before taking the road to Es Molins de sa Mirada.

6 Cala Saona

As the road climbs the small hill to the Sa Mirada windmill there are superb views back towards the lakes and the village. Continue to the end of the paved road, then take the track to the left. Follow the marked Green Route south for 2.5km (1½ miles) to Cala Saona.

By now you may feel the need for another refreshing dip and this sheltered bay provides the perfect backdrop.

7 Camí de ses Vinyes

Take the paved road back to Sant Francesc Xavier. Leave the village in the direction of Sant Ferran de ses Roques and you can choose one of two routes back to Es Pujols. The first, about 750m (½ mile) from the town, on the left, follows a track along the edge of the lagoon. Alternatively, turn right into Sant Ferran, looking out for the first unpaved road on your left. This is known locally as the Camí de ses Vinyes because it passes through an area of vineyards.

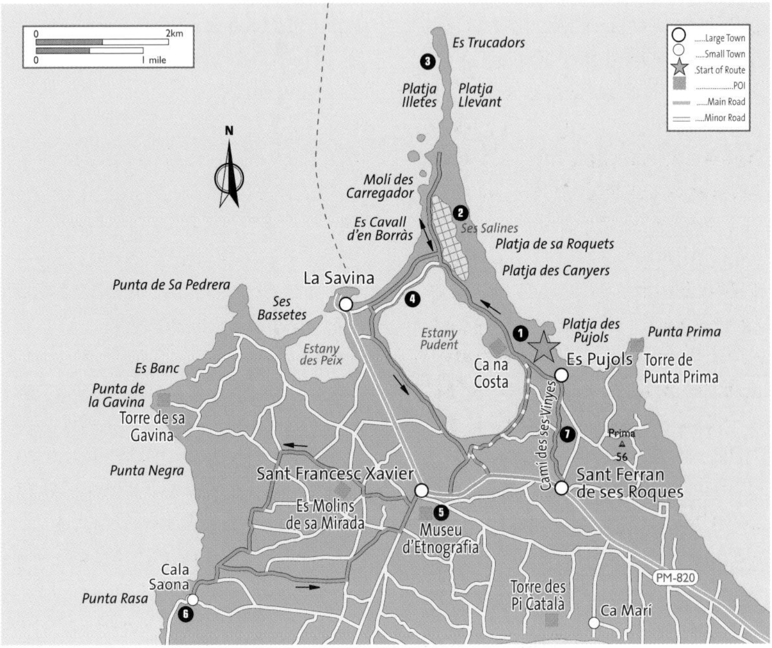

plovers, spotted redshank, great reed warblers and black-winged stilt. Estany Pudent was originally called Flamingo Lagoon, and a colony of these beautiful birds still breeds here, although numbers have been decreasing.

Outlying islands

Ibiza is separated from Formentera by the **Es Freus** channel. The scattered islands and the waters themselves together form part of the Ses Salines conservation area. Es Freus attracts numerous varieties of seabirds. Colonies of storm petrel, Audouin's and yellow-legged gulls and Balearic shearwater are now established on some of the islands, while fisher eagles and cormorants are also common around these waters. The first of the islets, just beyond the salt pans at Ses Salines, is **Illa d'es Penjats** (Island of the Hanged). The first prisoners to be executed here in 1271 were captured Berber pirates. To the west are two tiny islands, the **Illes Negres** (Black Islands), and beyond them, **Espalmador** (*see p125*). Off the coast of Espalmador are two islands: **Illa des Porcs** (Pig Island), which merits its own lighthouse – the channel can be particularly treacherous here – and **Illa des Torretes** (Turret Island), a reference to earlier defensive functions. Private yachts sometimes moor here, as there are good beaches. On the far side of Espalmador is **Espardell**. Goats pastured here in the past, only to be driven away by the harsh climate, but the rabbits proved to be made of sterner stuff. The endemic Pitiusan wall lizard breeds on Espardell and the island also supports a colony of cormorants.

No longer the preserve of goats, Espalmador has excellent swimming beaches

Hippies, including it is said Bob Dylan, once inhabited the windmills at El Pilar de la Mola

El Pilar de la Mola

The pine-wooded ascent from the Mar i Land end of Es Migjorn beach may be tough going but it is worth the effort for the spectacular views of Formentera and the south coast of Ibiza from **Es Mirador**. (Those with foresight will have booked a table on the terrace of the El Mirador restaurant, just off the main road – *see p169.*) In fact, the *mirador* is not the highest point on the island – that honour belongs to Sa Talaiassa at 202m (663ft), a little further to the east. Just beyond the hill is the plain of La Mola, where the fertile soil nurtures vines, wheat, figs, vegetables and other crops. The Augustinian monks who cleared the first tract of forest here back in the 13th century began this farming tradition, before falling victim to the Black Death. The hamlet of **El Pilar de la Mola** consists of little more than a few dozen houses clustering round a typical whitewashed parish church (1796). A congenial spot to linger over a drink, El Pilar comes into its own on Sunday afternoons for the craft market. Going after something authentic may be a wasted exercise, although there are local artisans from the hippy era still at work around here. One or two of them may

Far de la Mola – lighthouse at the end of the world

remember Bob Dylan, who lived on Formentera for a while in the 1960s. There is a story that he set up home in the old windmill (Molí Vell) near the village, which dates from 1778 and is still in working order.

From here the Sant Francesc road runs as straight as a die over the final 2km (1¼ miles) to **Far de la Mola**. This was the island's only lighthouse (until Far de Barbària was installed in the early 1970s), and in 1877 it provided the inspiration for the French science fiction writer Jules Verne's novel *Hector Servadac*. A granite monument reminds visitors of the fact. Rock sparrows find the barren terrain here congenial, while peregrine falcons make their nests in the cliffs. Fortunately, collectors no longer raid the ledges for birds' eggs – this was once such a common practice that it even gave rise to a verb, *virotar*, from the Eivissenc word *virot* (shearwater). South of Far de la Mola is Es Condolar, a small cove from where supplies of petrol would have been brought up to the lighthouse keeper – a practice which died out only around 50 years ago. To explore the south coast of the island from La Mola, pick up the Camí des Estufador at El Pilar de la Mola, which ends in a steep descent to **S'Estufador**. Along the way are the charcoal stacks (*estufas*) and lime kilns that give the place its name.

Platja de Migjorn

This stunning beach, one of the finest in the Pitiusas, begins 2.5km (1½ miles) east of Sant Ferran (take the side turning to Es Ca Marí). Arrive here and, stretching before you for the next 6km (4 miles), is an almost unbroken vista of dazzling white sand, dunes and pines.

Conveniently sited at the back of the beach are half a dozen excellent *chiringuitos* serving snacks and cold drinks. You could also check out the famous Blue Bar. Perched on a hillock to the west of Es Ca Marí is the **Torre de Migjorn** (also known as Torre des pi des Català), a watchtower that last saw action in 1813 when a party of French soldiers tried to land here but was repelled. A little further along the coast is an idyllic little spot called **Es Torrent de s'Alga** where the local fishermen mend their nets and lay out their catch in the sun to dry. The countryside behind the beach is typical of Formentera's central isthmus – wheat fields enclosed by drystone walls, fig trees, prickly pears (thought to discourage mosquitoes) and whitewashed houses, the trailing bougainvillea adding an extra dash of colour.

Punta de sa Gavina

A small country road from Estany des Peix leads to the headland of Punta de sa Gavina, from where there are marvellous views across the island to Espalmador, La Savina and the salt lagoons. A watchtower, **Torre de sa Gavina**, was erected here in the 18th century but never fitted with artillery.

Platja de Migjorn offers great facilities for beach lovers

Cycle ride: To La Mola

The following itinerary, from Sant Francesc Xavier to the eastern tip of the island, is about 15km (9 miles) one way and involves a steep climb to the thickly forested promontory of La Mola. As with the previous itinerary, it is designed with cyclists in mind and incorporates several of the suggested Green Routes.

Allow about 3½ hours without any stops.

1 Isthmus

Leave Sant Francesc Xavier on Calle Sant Jaume, by the Ethnographic Museum. At the edge of the town, where the road divides, take the right fork. This is part of the old road that runs through the centre of the low, sandy isthmus to the east of the peninsula. It follows a parallel course to the main road, which you join after passing the remains of a 3rd-century Roman camp at Can Pins (now no more than a heap of stones). After 1km

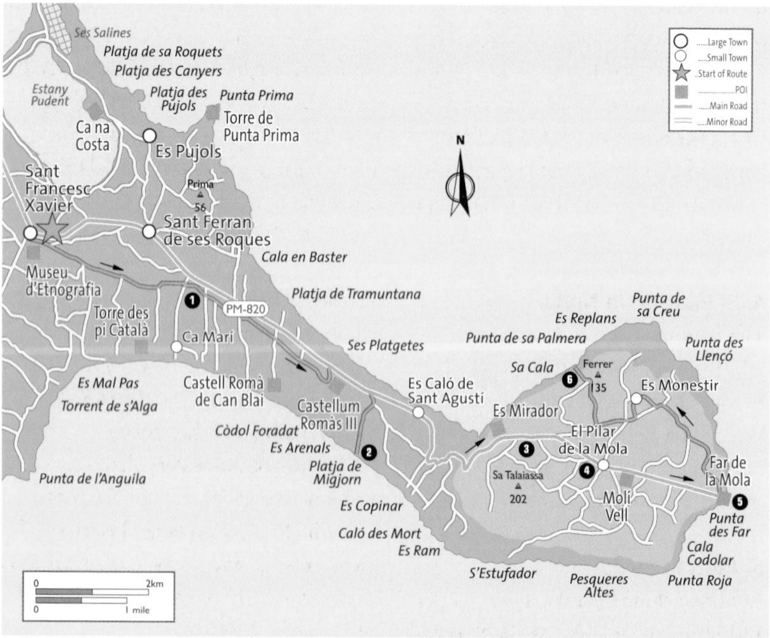

($^{2}/_{3}$ mile) take the track to the right through wheat fields, which give way to pine trees and sand dunes, as you approach Platja de Migjorn.

2 Platja de Migjorn

This sweeping crescent of dazzling white sand is characteristic of Formentera's unspoilt beaches. If you have worked up a thirst, there are a handful of excellent *chiringuitos* (snack shacks) to choose from.

3 Sa Talaiassa

Take any of the paths from the beach to return to the main road. Continue past the small fishing port of Es Caló de Sant Agustí and begin the climb to the plateau. Sa Talaiassa, the highest point on the island, at over 200m (650ft), is off to your right. This is a tough, steep, 1.5km (1-mile) ride, but the *mirador* at the 14km (9 miles) marker makes it worth the effort. As you stop to recover your breath, you can enjoy wonderful views across the bay of Sant Agustí and the isthmus.

4 El Pilar de la Mola

The road now descends to the tiny village of El Pilar de la Mola, which becomes surprisingly busy on Wednesday and Sunday evenings (summer only), when a small craft market is held in the square.

5 Punta des Far

Continue along the main road past the 18th-century Molí Vell, an old windmill still in working order. Three kilometres (2 miles) further on is Far de la Mola, a 102m (335ft) tall lighthouse that stands at the eastern tip of the island. Nearby is a monument to the French writer Jules Verne, who immortalised this 'lighthouse at the end of the world' in his book *Hector Servadac.*

Boardwalk leading to Platja de Migjorn

6 Sa Cala

If you have the time and are not too exhausted, take the right-hand track across the cliffs to Es Monestir, named after a 13th-century Augustinian monastery that was abandoned at the time of the Black Death (1348). Continue through agricultural land to the cliffs at Sa Cala, from where there are superb views of the north coastline.

Sant Ferran de ses Roques, Formentera's second town

Sant Ferran de ses Roques

Sant Ferran de ses Roques used to be closer to the salt lagoons, where most of the population made its living, but when the church fell into disrepair in the 1870s it was decided to relocate the town a little further inland. Most tourists make a beeline for **Fonda Pepe**, a bar that has nostalgic associations for hippies – Bob Dylan stayed there at one time. Mementoes of the era cover the walls, and such is the cachet of the place that you need to book a room long before you set out on holiday. Some ageing hippies still live in the area, eking out a living selling paintings and knick-knacks outside the church or on the square.

Sant Francesc Xavier

About 2km (1¼ miles) from La Savina, the tiny island capital (population 1,000) is a useful port of call if you need to use a post office, pharmacy or bank, but only worth a quick visit otherwise. Opposite the town hall on the main square is the **Església de Sant Francesc**. Built between 1726 and 1738, the church was fortified with cannon at one time, a necessary precaution as pirates were a menace as late as the middle of the 19th century. There is little to see inside, apart from a curious baptismal font by the main door. It predates the church by up to 1,000 years but its origins are shrouded in mystery. At a push one can make out oxen's heads and a human face among the faded sculptures.

The battered little community that lived in Sant Francesc Xavier during the Middle Ages worshipped in the **Capella de sa Tanca**. Built in the 14th century, it fell into disuse not long afterwards when the Black Death more or less finished off the island's beleaguered population. New colonists, arriving on Formentera at the end of the 17th century, restored the building, though it is so tiny that only a few of them would have been able to attend services. The most interesting exhibit in the **Museu d'Etnografia** (Ethnographic Museum) – the diminutive steam engine that hauled salt to the dock at La Savina – is outside.

If a sandy cove, sheltered from the wind by a pine-forested headland, sounds an attractive proposition at this point, cycle the 2.5km ($1^1/_2$-mile) Green Route to **Cala Saona**. More scenic than the main road, it also cuts the journey time in half. It is hard to credit, but a 16th-century map depicts a busy port at Cala Saona with anchorage for 400 ships. Earlier still, the falcons that bred on the cliffs were trained here for hunting.

Museu d'Etnografia. Open: summer Mon–Sat 10am–2pm & 7–9pm; winter 10.30am–1.30pm. Free admission.

Pretty as a picture – Plaça de sa Constitució, the main square in Sant Francesc Xavier

La Savina

Today, Formentera has only one port of entry, La (sometimes Sa) Savina. An island until the breakwater was constructed in the 1930s, the harbour was widened to accommodate cruise ships from Mallorca and the mainland. Ferries from Ibiza disembark at the quayside near the first of two yachting marinas, where you will also find the offices of diving schools and car and boat hire firms. Fishing trips are advertised and there are numerous bike rental outlets all offering reasonable rates. Hire a mountain bike if you aim to get as far as La Mola or the Barbària peninsula. The shops stay open until the last ferry has sailed so there is no rush to return cars or bikes. The best of the restaurants on the quayside is Aigüa but La Savina offers little else to detain the visitor. Buses to Sant Francesc, Sant Ferran, Es Pujols and La Mola depart from the stop near the tourist information office. There is a taxi rank here, too.

Es Trucadors peninsula

Hyperbole aside, the 3km (2-mile) spur extending to the northernmost point of Formentera deserves the description of Mediterranean paradise. Boat excursions to Espalmador from La Savina call at Ses Illetes, but the extraordinary beauty of Es Trucadors is best discovered on a bike (*see pp128–9*). Follow the Camí de Ses Illetes around the Estany Pudent lagoon, then take the

The harbour at La Savina is a hive of activity

Outside the high season Ses Illetes is all but deserted

signposted turning. Along the way are sublime views across the dunes, pines and salt pans which form part of the Ses Salines National Park, one of the most ecologically diverse regions in the Mediterranean. The road leads to the car park and a choice of two pristine beaches, equally devoid of urban development. On the western side of the promontory is **Platja Illetes**, which takes its name from the offshore islands of Pouet and Rodona – close enough to swim to if the sea is calm – while to the east is **Platja de Llevant**. As the distance between the two is never more than 200m (220yd) it's possible to beach hop. This idea isn't as crazy as it sounds because, owing to a quirk of nature, the onshore breezes affect only one side of the promontory at a time. While Es Trucadors is a popular destination at the height of the summer, it's always possible to find a space. *Chiringuitos* (snack shacks) are placed strategically along the beaches and are better value than the local restaurants. Anyone in a more adventurous frame of mind will find that water-skiing and other sports are available. Having got this far you may be tempted to reconnoitre the last stretch of the peninsula, but to do this you will have to leave the bikes behind. The track peters out at **Es Pas des Trucadors**, the straits separating Formentera from the island of Espalmador. The hardy plant (*herba des Trucadors*) which grows in the shallow water here is said to be good for curing stomach aches. The dunes are more fragile, sometimes disappearing altogether when the tide comes in.

Getting away from it all

It would be tempting to visit mainland Spain as its coastline is visible from one or two points on Ibiza on a clear day. There are direct sailings to Valencia and Dénia (there is an onward coach connection to Valencia from Dénia).

A visit to Mallorca not only provides a change of scene, but is an opportunity to discover the subtle differences between two Catalan cultures. Mallorca's capital is a lively city with a population of over 300,000.

Palma, Mallorca

There is a great deal to see, including a magnificent harbour, a glorious medieval cathedral, a Moorish castle, ruined Arab baths and a collection of superb aristocratic mansions dating from the 15th to the 19th centuries. Palma has a sophisticated cosmopolitan air and among its other attractions are excellent shopping and nightlife. There are two main tourist offices: at Estación Marítima, 2 and Plaça d'Espanya.

Getting there

The ferry company **Baleària** operates two services. The slow ferry leaves Eivissa at 2.45 on Mon, Wed, Sat & Sun and takes 4½ hours. The fast service (2 hours) departs daily at 8pm. Return services from Palma leave (slow) Mon–Sat at 10am and Sun at 9am, and (fast) daily at 8am.
Tel: (902) 16 01 80;
www.balearia.com

Trasmediterránea high-speed ferries depart from Eivissa for Palma Mon, Wed, Sat & Sun in summer at 7pm (journey time 2 hours and 45 min). Ferries from Palma returning to Eivissa depart Mon, Wed, Sat & Sun at 7pm.
Tel: (902) 45 46 45;
www.trasmediterranea.es

Times vary in winter. Realistically, visiting Palma from Ibiza involves a stay of a couple of nights. *See p179 for accommodation options.*

La Seu (Cathedral)

One of the jewels of Spanish Gothic architecture, work on Palma's pinnacled cathedral was begun in the 13th century, shortly after the Christian Reconquest. The building was restored in the early 1900s by the great Catalan architect Antoni Gaudí. Special points of interest include the stunning stained glass (the cathedral boasts the largest rose window in the world), the wrought-iron baldachino by Gaudí above the main altar, and the museum with its displays of precious religious objects and Gothic art works.

La Seu, Palma's great cathedral soars above the harbour

Plaça d'Almoina. Open: Apr–Oct Mon–Fri 10am–5.15pm (until 6.15pm June–Sept), Sat 10am–2.15pm; Nov–Mar Mon–Fri 10am–3.15pm, Sat 10am–2.15pm. Admission charge.

Palau de l'Almudaina

This imposing building was originally the palace of the Moorish governors of the city and was subsequently adapted for use by the Christian rulers of Mallorca. It is still one of the official residences of the king and queen of Spain. The remains of the **Banys Arabs** (Arab Baths), lost in the picturesque warren of streets behind the cathedral, are another reminder of the Moorish presence in the city.

Palace, Carrer del Palau Reials. Tel: 971 72 71 34. Open for guided tours Apr–Sept Mon–Fri 10am–6pm, Sat 10am–2pm; Oct–Mar Mon–Fri 10am–2pm & 4–6pm. Admission charge.

Arab Baths, Carrer Can Serra 7. Tel: 971 72 15 49. Open: Apr–Nov daily 9.30am–7.30pm; Dec–Mar 9.30am–6pm. Admission charge.

Fundació Pilar i Joan Miró

The home and studio of one of Spain's most innovative modern artists contains more than 100 of his paintings, as well as sculptures and other works.

Carrer Joan de Saridakis 29, Cala Major. Tel: 971 70 14 20. Open: mid-May–mid-Sept Tue–Sat 10am–7pm, Sun 10am–3pm; mid-Sept–mid-May Tue–Sat 10am–6pm, Sun 10am–3pm.

A visit to the Spanish mainland

Getting there

The **Balearia** fast ferry to Dénia leaves Eivissa daily at 11am and arrives 2 hours later. The coach connection from Dénia to Valencia takes an extra 1 hour 15 minutes. The fast ferry returning to Eivissa departs daily at 5pm. There is another ferry departing from Sant Antoni daily at 8.30pm in summer. Again allow the extra time for the onward journey to Valencia. Check the website for timings to and from Ibiza as only one or two ferries run daily.

Tel: (902) 16 01 80; www.balearia.com

Times vary in winter. The trip to Dénia could be done as a day excursion, but the Valencia extension necessitates an overnight stay. *See p179 for accommodation options.*

The **Trasmediterránea** high-speed ferry leaves Eivissa for Valencia Sat and Sun at 10am in summer and takes approximately 3 hours. Ferries from Valencia to Eivissa depart Fri and Sat at 5pm in summer. Times vary in winter.

Tel: (902) 45 46 45; www.trasmediterranea.es

Dénia

This bustling port has a rich history and culture dating back to Carthaginian times. Near the port is a delightful old quarter of cobbled streets and trim, whitewashed

The medieval Catedral de Valencia

buildings. The main sight, the 16th-century castle, dominates the town. Dénia has some great tapas bars and seafood restaurants on the waterfront, and the cafés on the main street, Calle Marqués de Campo, are also worth checking out. The **Costa del Azahar** is a region of beautiful beaches, mostly Blue Flag. An alternative to Dénia itself is the charming resort of **Jávea** (easily reached by taxi). The sands here were immortalised in the work of the Spanish artist Joaquín Sorolla at the beginning of the 20th century, and the attractive hillside village merits a look. Dénia's tourist information office (*www.denia.net*) is on Plaza Oculista Buigues 9. *Tel: (966) 42 23 67.*

Valencia

Spain's third-largest city (population around 800,000) is a thriving port, renowned for its nightlife. Its history dates back to Roman times, and there is a great deal to see in and around the crumbling **Barrio del Carmen.** The most arresting Gothic monument is the beautifully proportioned **Lonja de los Mercaderes** (Silk Exchange). There are wonderful views of the city from the top of the tower of Valencia's **Cathedral**, also medieval in origin. The huge glass and wrought-iron **Mercado Central** (Central Market) is one of the largest in Europe and showcases Spain's most productive market garden region. Also worth a look is the **Museu de Belles Artes** (Fine

Good seafood is a Spanish institution

The old centre of Valencia is an engaging mix of architectural styles

Arts Museum), with works by El Greco, Hieronymus Bosch, Velázquez and Goya, and the relatively new **Ciudad de las Artes y las Ciencias** (City of Arts and Sciences), a major architectural landmark, built in the late 1990s, which includes a concert hall, IMAX cinema, science museum and the largest aquarium in Europe (Parque Oceanográfico). Cafés and restaurants abound in the streets to the south of the cathedral. Valencia is the home of paella, but you should also try *fideúa* (seafood and noodles cooked paella-style). In the summer the refreshing non-alcoholic drink *horchata*, made from tiger nuts and best served *granizada* (with ice), is an excellent thirst-quencher. The tourist information office is on Plaza de la Reina.
Tel: (963) 15 39 31; *www.turisvalencia.es*

Shopping

While books, DVDs, personal stereos, computers and kitchen equipment are more expensive in Spain than in northern Europe, most other items, including clothes, shoes, CDs and a lot of foodstuffs, are still competitively priced. Most tourist shops offer tax-free shopping for non-EU residents.

WHAT TO BUY

A creation of the 1970s, the Ad Lib 'look' has been the height of Spanish chic and gained international attention on the fashion circuit. Traditional handicrafts have taken a bit of a pummelling from foreign competition, but if you look hard enough you can still find genuine, high-quality pottery and ceramics, embroidery, basket weaving, tapestries, leather goods, espadrilles, traditional folk instruments and the local liqueur, *Hierbas Ibicencas.* During the summer, craft fairs and markets are held at various locations around the islands – look out for advertisements or check with the nearest tourist office for details.

AD LIB

This uniquely Ibizan fashion phenomenon took off in the early 1970s, a few years after Smilja Mijailovich, a Serbian-born princess, opened the first clothing store with the Ad Lib label (from the Latin *ad libitum,* meaning 'anything goes'). Drawing her inspiration from traditional folk costumes and the 'dressing-down' styles of Ibizan hippies, she and her fellow designers combined plain white fabrics such as cotton and calico with bright colours. The Ibiza 'look', also characterised by revealing, flouncy bodices, low-slung leather belts and wooden sandals, has enjoyed a new lease of life, thanks to the interest of fashion-conscious celebrities like Claudia Schiffer and Penélope Cruz.

WHERE TO SHOP

In Eivissa, head to Dalt Vila for Ad Lib clothing and accessories, antiques and modern art. The clothing stores and boutiques of La Marina and Sa Penya (especially on Carrer Mare de Déu and Carrer Major) also stock Ad Lib fashions and are an excellent source for clubbing outfits. For general shopping, start with Passeig Vara de Rey then move on to the busy streets of the new town, especially Bartolomeu Rosselló, Isidor Macabich and Ignasi Wallis. This is where the locals shop, so prices are more competitive than in the tourist areas.

Art and antiques

While you're unlikely to find genuine antiquities for sale anywhere in the Pitiusas, you will find an interesting assortment of 19th- and 20th-century books, furniture, paintings and curios. The work of dozens of contemporary artists living on the islands is also available and well worth a browse.

Casi Todo

Sales take place regularly at this English-owned auction house whose name means 'almost everything', and where indeed you can find everything from vintage motorbikes to grandfather clocks.

Santa Gertrudis. www.casitodo.com

Paco Polenghi

The old Carl van der Voort gallery is under new ownership and sells high-quality and expensive art. The gallery specialises in 20th-century and contemporary paintings, sculptures and original prints.

Plaça de la Vila 15, Dalt Vila, Eivissa.

Art for sale in Es Canar Hippy Market

Bookshops

Lavish art or coffee-table books are, on the whole, more expensive here than in northern Europe, although there is the occasional bargain to be had. Books on Ibiza and Formentera abound and make good souvenirs. Several bookstores have foreign-language sections for anyone missing a good read.

Libro Azul
Stocks a comprehensive range of books on the islands. Also specialises in architecture and design, photography and culture. And there's a café.
Sa Nova Gertrudis, Santa Gertrudis.

Clothing and boutiques

Arizona
Exclusive, made-to-measure, quality leather fashions from a workshop founded in 1983.
Carrer Castelar 17, Eivissa.

Beatriz Leyon
Leather jackets and accessories.
Passeig Vara del Rey 12, Eivissa.

Boutique Divina
Ad Lib *haute couture* for men, women and children, at prices to match.
Plaça de la Vila 17, Eivissa.

Cantonada
One of the longest-established Ad Lib outlets on the island. Off-the-peg day and evening wear in natural fabrics and light or warm colours.
Carrer Comte de Rosselló 10, New Town, Eivissa.

Casa Afro
This shop sells typical Ibizenco-style jewellery and watches.
Carrer Comte de Roselló 8, Eivissa

DET DET
Some outlandish creations sit side by side more demure cotton dresses; all Scandinavian-designed.
Carrer Bisbe Azara 4, Eivissa

Harvey Musin
This shop sells beautiful, soft and light linen dresses and colourful summer clothing.
Plaça de la Constitució 7, Eivissa.

Ibiza Republic Boutique
Famous for its star within a circle logo, designer Bernadette Loriot's store is the height of Ibiza cool. Shop here for tops, dresses, wraps, swimwear, jogging gear and sandals. English-speaking staff.
Carrer de la Creu 25, Eivissa.

ONNA
This shop sells mainly handbags in all forms, shapes and sizes. Also beach and fashion clothing.
Josep Verdera 17, Eivissa.

PACHA
Shop on the waterfront selling the latest trends for clubbing.
Platja, Santa Eulària des Riu.

Sandal Shop
Everything for the leather enthusiast – handmade bags, belts, sandals, boots – though at a price.
Plaça de la Vila 2, Eivissa.

Te Cuero
All kinds of leather goods, but mainly handbags and accessories.
Plaça de la Església, Santa Eulària.

Food and drink

When you've done shopping for Ibizan liqueurs, pause to investigate the spirits and Spanish wines. The prices will bowl you over.

Bodega Ribas

Second-generation business specialising in quality Spanish wines and liqueurs (including *Hierbas Ibicencas*). Also a selection of champagnes, all at competitive prices.

Carrer Sant Vicent 18 (just off Plaça d'Espanya), Santa Eulària.

Simple cotton clothing on sale in Ibiza Town

Casa Alfonso

Useful downtown off-licence with excellent deli section.

Progrès 8. Corner of Sant Antoni and Carrer Ample (behind Marina), Sant Antoni.

Eivissa Ecolandia

Everything you need for healthy eating. This health-food supermarket has an extensive selection of organic fruit and vegetables, wine, beer, cereals, milk, Ibizan honey and fresh bread for sale.

Avda Dr Fleming 37, Sant Antoni.

Marí Mayans

Official outlet of the leading distiller of Ibizan herb liqueurs since 1880. *Hierbas ibicencas* is flavoured with aniseed, thyme, rosemary, lemon and orange peel, but you should also try *palo* (drunk as an aperitif with a few drops of gin added) and *frígola*, a drier Ibizan liqueur. Marí Mayans is also renowned for its absinthe.

Carrer V Marí Mayans 19–21, Puig d'en Valls, Santa Eulària; www.marimayans.com. Also Eivissa and Sant Antoni.

Thomas Green

An English supermarket claiming to sell 'the best of British'.

Camí des Moli, Block 8, Sant Antoni de Portmany. www.tgibiza.com

Records and CDs

As you might expect from Europe's clubbing capital, there are a number of excellent record stores stocking vinyl and CD dance mixes. Start your search at one of the following:

Discos Delta
Creu 32, Eivissa.

Discos Prava
General Prim 4, Sant Antoni.

Souvenirs

Ceramiques Es Test
You will find jars, figures and other ceramic *objets* from local craftsmen.
Carrer Mar 15, Eivissa.

Groch
International perfumes at reduced prices, as well as Spanish and Ibizan fragrances. Also on sale are bags, belts and other fashion accessories.
Punta Arabí end of Es Canar beach, Santa Eulària des Riu.

El Paraiso
Lladró porcelain is not to everyone's taste, but if you are a fan you'll find prices considerably lower here than in northern Europe. At the last count, this

Ceramics are the speciality of Sant Rafel

outlet stocked more than 1,000 figurines, including limited editions. It also sells cut glass.
Carrer M Riquer Wallis (near the beach), Santa Eulària des Riu.

Sports shops

Deportes El Coral
Large sports stockists with a comprehensive range of clothing, shoes and equipment.
Carrer Sant Antoni 23, Sant Antoni.

Craft markets

Ibiza is famous for its hippy markets, though you'll be lucky to find much in the way of authentic handicrafts nowadays. If you're on the lookout for a sarong or a tie-dye shirt, on the other hand, look no further.

Eivissa. By the port. *Open: daily in the afternoon in summer.*

El Pilar de la Mola, Formentera. Art market in the central square. Locally made jewellery and handicrafts.
Open: May–Sept Wed & Sun.

Club Punta Arabí – Es Canar. The best-known market (*see pp60–61*). *Open: Wed in summer 8am–6pm.*

San Miguel
Handicrafts for sale in the village square.
Open: Thur 6–8pm (May–Oct).

Sant Carles – Las Dalias. Arguably the best of the bunch, with an excellent selection of clothes and jewellery.
Open: Sat all day, all year round.

Sant Jordi. At the hippodrome.

Attention-grabbing designs are a feature of Ibizan leatherware

Second-hand and hippy market.
Open: Sat all year round.

Santa Eulària des Riu.
A small line of stalls on the main street, Passeig de S'Alamera.
Open: daily summer.

Entertainment

Essentially, entertainment in Ibiza is its nightclubs and bars. These range from terraces with captivating sea views to old hippy haunts, tapas bars, chill-out and beach bars. Most are open all day and until late (at least 1am). The best areas to head for in Eivissa are La Marina and Sa Penya, though Dalt Vila is also worth checking out, and, of course, the beaches – especially Platja d'en Bossa – in summer.

The best bars in Sant Antoni are in the area known as Sunset Strip, on the way to Caló des Moro. Santa Eulària is not known for its nightlife, but does have one disco-bar, Guaraná. Technically, the clubbing season begins at the beginning of June but actually takes a week or two to get under way. Thereafter it's all go until the end of September. Only two clubs, Pacha and El Divino, remain open during winter, when there are substantial price reductions.

BARS

Benniràs

Chiringuito

A relaxed, rustic bar on the beach at Benniràs that gets going around sunset with pre-clubbing drinkers.
Benniràs, on the northwest coast.
Open: noon until late.

Cala Jondal

Blue Marlin

A very cool bar where mist is sprayed from the walls when it gets too hot.
Tel: 971 41 01 17. Open: May–Oct.
www.bluemarlinibiza.com

Eivissa

Km 5

Km 5 is one of the hippest venues on the island. The resident DJs play cutting-edge funk, house and techno music. Dancing continues until late, and the vegetarian food is good, too.
Carretera Sant Josep 5.6km.
Tel: 971 39 63 49;
www.km5-lounge.com.
Open: Apr–Oct nightly 8pm–4am.

La Muralla

Friendly and extremely popular gay bar in the heart of Dalt Vila, with a small outdoor terrace.
Sa Carrossa 3, Dalt Vila, Eivissa.
Tel: 971 30 18 83;
www.lamuralla-ibiza.com.
Open: Easter–Nov.

Mao Rooms

An über-swanky offering from the Chinawhite stable, where the beautiful

people lie on daybeds in an African-inspired interior.
Carrer d'Emili Pou 6.
Open: 10.30pm until late.

Rock Bar
Something of a local institution, the Rock Bar is a favourite place for fashionistas to go for a pre-club drink.
Carrer Cipriano Carijo 14.

Sunset Café
Café bar on one of Eivissa's quieter squares, perfect for leafing through the newspaper over a leisurely breakfast.
Plaça des Parc 8. Tel: 971 39 44 46.

Teatro Pereira
Though no longer a theatre, the first neocolonial-style building in Eivissa is still a major live music venue hosting regular jazz concerts. The café stays open until 5am during the summer.
Carrer Comte Rosselló 3.
Tel: 971 19 48 68. Open: all year.

Zoo Bar
Another long-standing bar in the port area. Drop in for a drink and to pick up discount club flyers.
Passeig Marítim. www.zooibiza.com

Formentera

Blue Bar
Formentera's answer to the sunset bars on Ibiza, the Blue Bar is a chilled-out bar and restaurant with cocktails and DJs.
Platja de Migjorn.

San José

Kumharas
A mix of bar, restaurant and performance space, Kumharas is distinctly alternative. Enjoy the sunset and one of the many musical events from the terrace.
Carrer Lugo 2, Cala de Bou; www.kumharas.org. Open: 10am–midnight.

Sant Antoni de Portmany

Bar M
M for Manumission, the promoters who own the bar. Across the road from Es Paradis, this pre-clubbing venue is especially popular with the British.
Avda Dr Fleming. Open: May–Oct.

Café del Mar
The original sunset bar, this was also the birthplace of the chill-out compilation. Arrive before 7pm to be sure of a seat, or sit out on the rocks and admire the view.
Sunset Strip (Carrer Vara de Rey).
Tel: 971 34 25 16.
www.cafedelmarmusic.com.
Open: Apr–Oct.

Café Mambo
Another sunset bar; DJs and promoters also like to drop in here after Café del Mar has closed for the night. Famous for its pre-club parties featuring guest DJs.
Sunset Strip (Carrer Vara de Rey).
Tel: 971 34 66 38;
www.cafemamboibiza.com.
Open: May–Oct 11am–4am.

Coastline
Although it is essentially a bar, Coastline also has a restaurant, a shop, no fewer than three swimming pools and a sun terrace.
Badia de Sant Antoni. Tel: 971 34 85 53; www.coastlinecafe.com

Kanya

Popular with sunset-watchers and house music enthusiasts, this bar-restaurant (Thai food) has a large pool and terrace. Dancing until 4am, licence permitting, but the drinks are expensive.

Carrer Soledad 53.
www.ibiza-kanya.com

Sant Carles de Peralta

Anita's Bar

A hippy haunt back in the 1970s, Anita's is still going strong, thanks to its warm atmosphere and good pub grub.

Sant Carles village (look for the sign near the bus stop).

Las Dalias

Las Dalias is a venue for special events, usually of the psychedelic variety. Tapas are served in the bar (open until 2.30am).

Ctra Santa Eulària–Sant Carles 12km. Tel: 971 32 68 25; www.lasdalias.com

Sant Joan de Labritja

ECO Centre

'New-Age Bazaar', bar and Internet café with a pleasant garden. Closes 9pm.

Plaça de Espanya 5.
Tel: 971 33 30 29;
www.eco-ibiza.com

Santa Agnès de Corona

Can Cosmi

Typical village bar with a great atmosphere, a terrace overlooking the church and down-to-earth prices.

Santa Agnès. Tel: 971 80 50 20.
Closed: Tue.

Santa Eulària des Riu

Guaraná

A bar that hosts a wide range of guest DJs playing everything from Brazilian to Blues. Some live performances.

Port Esportiu. www.guaranaibiza.com.
Open: until 6am.

Santa Gertrudis de Fruitera

Bar Costa

Spanish cured hams (*jamón serrano*) dangle from the roof before being sliced and served up in mouthwatering *bocadillos* (bread rolls) and *tostadas.*

Plaça de l'Església. Tel: 971 19 70 21.

CLUBS

When going clubbing, most visitors pay at the door, although it is cheaper and more convenient to pick up an advance ticket (available online at *www.ibiza-spotlight.com*). Prices are high (anything from €60, depending on the season and what's on) and on top of that there are the drinks – a bottle of water can set you back another €6. Some fliers offer a price reduction and/or a free drink. People start arriving at bars for pre-club drinks at around midnight and head off to the clubs around 1.30am. Generally speaking, there are no dress codes – only football shirts and beachwear are unacceptable. Sleeping on the beach is illegal, and drink-driving laws are rigorously enforced, with spot checks commonplace. While drugs like ecstasy are widely available, they are illegal and the police will decide whether what you are carrying is for personal consumption or with the intention of dealing.

Amnesia

The latest improvements to this club have further improved the quality of the sound system and the bass is now said to be able to mimic in the human body sensations comparable to a massage. It hosts the famous Foam Party.

Ctra Eivissa–Sant Antoni 5km. Tel: 971 19 80 41; www.amnesia.es

Anfora

One of the oldest gay venues in Ibiza is in a natural cave and attracts an international mixed-age crowd.

Carrer Sant Carles 7, Dalt Vila, Eivissa. Tel: 971 30 28 93; www.disco-anfora.com. Open: May–mid-Oct.

El Divino

Opened in 1992 as a private club, this popular venue has evolved to become one of the most famous locations for international parties. Quality house music for a classy crowd.

Port Esportiu, Passeig Marítim, Eivissa. Tel: 971 31 83 38; www.eldivino-ibiza.com

Eden

This enormous two-storey disco with 13 bars in the port of Sant Antoni boasts a spectacular atmosphere. It incorporates two VIP areas, a back room and the obligatory chill-out area.

Carrer Salvador Espriu, Sant Antoni. Tel: 971 80 32 40; www.edenibiza.com

Pacha

The epitomy of Ibiza clubbing – the cognoscenti say 'Pacha is Ibiza and Ibiza is Pacha' – is located near the Passeig Marítim which makes it easy to walk there from the port. To confirm its fame, international celebrities are often spotted here.

Avda 8 d'Agost, Passeig Marítim, Eivissa. Tel: 971 31 23 60; www.pacha.com

Es Paradis

The queen of discos in Sant Antoni opened its doors in 1975 and quickly became one of the focal points of the island's nightlife. The pyramid roof opens up at sunrise to let the sun in and tell clubbers that the night is finished. The spectacular decorations and the lush vegetation make it, some would say, the most beautiful disco in the world. It hosts the famous Water Party.

Carrer Salvador Espriu 2, Sant Antoni. Tel: 971 34 60 00; www.esparadis.com

Privilege

The world's biggest club has an indoor swimming pool and terraces with bay windows offering beautiful views of Ibiza. It stages erotic and artistic live performances and has a very good restaurant.

Ctra Eivissa–Sant Antoni 6km. Tel: 971 19 8086; www.privilegeibiza.com

Space

Located on the beach in Sant Josep, this club holds fantastic parties on different themes each day of the week, culminating with the popular 'We love Space' party on Sundays.

Sant Josep de sa Talaia. Tel: 971 39 67 93; www.space-ibiza.es

Children

Ibiza is a child-friendly destination where the biggest attraction is the numerous beaches with soft sand, gently shelving beaches and shallow, clear water. Some of the best bucket-and-spade resorts are on the east coast: Cala Llonga and Es Canar can both be reached by boat from Santa Eulària, and the ferry ride adds to the enjoyment.

Aquarium

Aquario Cap Blanc

Some boat excursions from Sant Antoni include a stop at this natural cave, now an aquarium. Half the pleasure for children lies in the illuminated grotto setting. Turtles, lobsters, octopuses, rays, wrasse, moray eels and other Balearic marine species swim in the shallow waters of the cave floor, while the youngsters look down from a wooden walkway.

Ten minutes' walk from Cala des Moro (take the path from Hotel Tanit). Open: Apr–Oct daily 10am–sunset.

Bowling Centre

A large complex in the shopping area of Platja d'en Bossa. The facilities include a four-lane bowling alley with mini-golf, trampolines and a safety-controlled mechanical bull thrown in.

Carrer Murtra 2–4, Platja d'en Bossa. Tel: 971 30 03 56.

Can Marça Cave

(*See pp79–80.*)

Clothing

Laly's Nens

Boutique designed specifically with children in mind. Has a large and varied selection of designer clothes by Oilily, Versace and the like.

Joan d'Austria/corner of Carrer Madrid, New Town, Eivissa.

Go-karting

A fun activity for adults as well as children of all ages. There are two circuits in Ibiza: one in Sant Antoni, the other in Santa Eulària. Both have twin-engined adult karts, junior karts, electric baby karts and bikes. Of the two tracks, Santa Eulària has the more attractive setting.

Go-Kart Santa Eulària

Also table football and games machines.

Ctra de Santa Eulària des Riu 5.7km. Tel: 971 31 77 44. Open: Apr–Oct daily 10am–9pm. Nov–Mar weekends and holidays from 11am.

Karting San Antonio

Family karts and floodlit at night.

Ctra Sant Antoni 14km, Sant Antoni. Tel: 971 34 38 05. Open: daily 10am–10pm.

Horse riding

There are horse-riding schools in Ibiza and Formentera, offering tuition for children and adults and excursions through lovely rural settings.

Escuela de Equitación Can Mayans
Santa Gertrudis/Sant Llorenç road. Tel: 971 18 73 88.

Paintball

Ibizaventura
Fun for older children shooting paints at each other. Minimum of six people, lasts 1 hour.
Avinguda Es Caló, St Josep de Sa Talaia. Tel: (653) 64 65 50; www.ibizaventura.com

Playground

Family entertainment centre behind Cala de Bou beach, with bouncy castle, trampolenes, mini-go-karts, boats and a playground. For the adults there's an amusement complex with ten-pin bowling, café and bars.
Camí des Molí, Bahía de Sant Antoni.

Scenic train

An open-top tourist train departs from the bus stop by The Egg in Sant Antoni on a two-hour excursion into the scenic countryside around Santa Agnès de la Corona, where there is a stop for a drink. The train then continues to a nearby *mirador* for great views. There is a similar trip from Santa Eulària.

Waterpark

Aguamar
The island's largest waterpark is just 100m (330ft) from the beach at Platja d'en Bossa. Apart from some spectacular rides, there is also a special picnic area, shop and café.
Platja d'en Bossa, Sant Josep de sa Talaia. Tel: 971 39 57 82. Open: May–Oct daily 10am–6pm.

Ibiza's caves were once used as smugglers' dens

Sport and leisure

Ibiza offers a wide variety of outdoor and leisure activities, from hiking and horse riding to canoeing and ballooning. Watersports enthusiasts are particularly well catered for, with schools on most of the main beaches offering tuition and equipment hire. If the listings below do not include your favourite sport, consult the tourist offices in Eivissa and La Savina (Formentera).

Balloon flights

Minimum of two, maximum of six people, approximately 40-min flight. Allow four hours for transportation from hotel, tuition and snack.
Tel: (630) 41 01 67; www.ibizaenglobo.com

Boat charter and fishing trips

Boats Ibiza
This company organises day trips and excursions and it has catamarans and yachts to rent.
Port, Sant Antoni. Mob: 663 745 520; www.boatsibiza.com

Navega Ibiza
Organises group excursions for a maximum of nine people to the north of the island and further afield. Yachts, catamarans and other boats are also available to hire.
Tel (mobile): 695 57 66 22; www.navegaibiza.com

Pesca Ibiza
Deep-sea fishing trips offered on a half-day basis.
Edifici Bristol, Avda 8 d'Agost, Eivissa. Tel: 971 31 44 91.

Tagomago Charters
Boats and skippers for hire.
Port Esportiu, Santa Eulària. Tel: 971 33 81 26.

Cycling

Elektracar
One good way to get around Formentera is by rechargeable electric bike. The shop also hires normal bikes and has accessories for children.
Carrer Almadrava, Edifici Auba, local B-3, La Savina. Tel: 971 32 28 75; www.elektracar.com

Ibiza Sport
Bicycles, including mountain bikes for rent. It also arranges excursions and accommodation and provides guides and support vehicles to carry the luggage.
Sant Antoni de Portmany. Tel: 971 34 74 56; www.ibizasport.com

Trolling for game fish off Eivissa

Diving schools

Most schools offer introductory PADI-approved courses. All equipment is included in the price.

Active Dive

All-year-round diving trips and courses.
Paseo Maritimo, Sant Antoni de Portmany.
Tel: 971 34 13 44; www.active-dive.com

Ibiza Diving College

Located on the Playa del Arenal beach, this diving school offers all levels of tuition and also provides PADI licences.
Playa del Arenal, Sant Antoni.
www.ibiza-diving-college.com

Punta Dive

The island's biggest diving company has a special programme for beginners, covering both the theory and practice of diving, with one instructor for every two students.
Cala Martina. Tel: 971 33 67 26;
www.puntadive.com

Subfari

Located in Portinatx, on the north of the island, this diving club enjoys one of the prettiest and most unspoiled locations of the island.
Puerto de Portinatx, San Joan de Labritja. Tel: 971 33 75 58;
www.subfari.es

LA RUTA DE LA SAL

This famous annual yachting event began in 1846 when merchant seamen transporting salt from Ibiza to the mainland held a race. More than 2,000 competitors and 300 vessels now take part in the race. Before the regatta, which takes place in April, boats are divided into categories – classic, vintage, multihull, etc. Some set off from Barcelona, others from Dénia, but all end up crossing the finishing line in Eivissa harbour.

Vellmari Diving Centre
Marina Botafoc, Eivissa.
Tel: 971 19 28 84.
Also at *La Savina, Formentera.*
Tel: 971 32 21 05; www.vellmari.com

Golf

For information about golf on the island contact the Balearic Island Golf Federation.
Tel: 971 72 27 53; www.fbgolf.com

Hiking

EcoIbiza
Organises treks to some of the more out-of-the-way spots on the island. Half day or full day.
Edifici Transat, Passeig Marítim local 10, Eivissa. Tel: 971 30 23 47; www.ecoibiza.com

Horse riding

Scenic excursions following coastal paths or into the woodland and hills of Ibiza and across the salt flats in Formentera.

Can Cirer
Ctra Sant Antoni-Santa Inés, Sant Antoni. Tel: 971 34 15 54.

Com Mayans
Carretera Santa Gertrudis – Sant Llorenç, Sta. Eulària. Tel: 908 636 884.

Easy Rider
Camí Camping, Cala Llonga.
Tel: 971 19 65 11.

Tennis

Club de Campo
Six clay tennis courts, and one squash court, all of which are floodlit. There's also a gym, sauna, swimming and a snack bar.
Ctra Sant Josep 4km.
Tel: 971 30 00 88.

Sun Active Tennis Club
This local Sant Antoni tennis club is located 7 minutes from town centre and has professional facilities and a tropical garden.
Cami Es Regueró, Sant Antoni de Portmany. Tel: 971 80 31 31; www.tennisibiza.com

Watersports

Cesar's Watersports
Hires out jet skis and organises parasailing, banana rides, water-skiing, and also boat hire.
Platja de S'Argamassa.
Tel: 971 33 09 19.

Club Nàutic
Tuition, social club and restaurant.
Moll Pesquer, Eivissa.
Tel: 971 31 33 63;
www.clubnauticoibiza.com.

Formentera Diving and Watersports
The best place here for diving tuition, kayak and jet-ski rental, and boat hire.
Marina de La Savina, Formentera.
Tel: 971 32 32 32.

Ibikayak
Courses of kayaking in the sea all year round. Also personalised excursions to Formentera for experienced kayakers, for individuals or groups up to a maximum of 5 people.
Tel (mobile): 647 95 31 68;
www.ibikayak.com

Ibiza Wake

A company located behind the hotel San Remo, on Playa S'Estanyol, which organises all kinds of water sports including wakeboard, flyfish, twister, jet ski, parasailing, and scubadiving.
Playa S'Estanyol. Tel: 971 34 55 22; www.ibizawake.com

There are **water-skiing** schools on more than a dozen Ibizan beaches, including: Platja d'en Bossa, Ses Salines, Cala d'Hort, Caló des Moro, Port de Sant Miquel, Cala Llonga and Es Canar.

There are **jet-ski** schools on the following beaches: Es Figueral, d'en Bossa, S'Argamassa, Sant Vicent and the river beach in Santa Eulària.

Yoga

Ibiza Yoga

Specialises in Ashtanga yoga, with some high-profile instructors. Offers retreats pre-booked from the UK, rather than drop-in classes.
Cala Bennirràs.
Tel: (UK 0044) 020 7419 0999;
www.ibizayoga.com.
Open: May–Oct.

Sunset over the Mediterranean from Cala Benniràs beach (*see p78*)

Food and drink

While Ibiza is not known for its gastronomy, it is possible to eat well on the island. The more sophisticated restaurants offer the best of Basque, Provençal and Catalan cuisine, while the more homely establishments specialise in rich and nourishing local dishes.

What to eat

Ibizan cooking is closely related to that of the other Balearic Islands, where traditionally the inhabitants had to make do with simple, often scarce ingredients. Soups and stews are the mainstays, drawing on the produce of the land and sea and generously seasoned with herbs and spices.

Where and when to eat

The main meal of the day is lunch (*el almuerzo*), eaten at around 2pm, more often than not in a café or restaurant. Virtually every establishment offers a *menú del día*, a great-value fixed-price, three-course meal including a drink. Typically, the choice of first courses will include a salad, a soup or two and possibly a paella; the second is a small selection of meat and fish dishes, followed by dessert – usually *flan* (crème caramel), rice pudding, fresh fruit or ice cream. If this sounds a bit much, look out for the list of *platos combinados*, one-course dishes which often include a drink or a side salad in the price. Dinner (*cena*) is comparatively light and will not be eaten until around 10pm. A group of friends will often dispense with a formal meal in favour of sharing *tapas* – small plates of appetisers served at the counter in bars. The custom is to visit several bars, sampling a *tapa* or two in each. After a night at a club, Spaniards like to finish off with an early breakfast of *chocolate con churros*, a cup of thick hot chocolate served with long thin doughnuts for dipping into the drink. When dining out, it is a good idea to book a table, at least in the more popular restaurants. The same goes for lunch on Sundays and public holidays when Spaniards eat out *en famille.* Kitchens close around midnight in Ibiza but considerably earlier in Formentera (as a rule, bars also shut much earlier here, at least in the villages). VAT (IVA in Spanish) of 8 per cent is added to restaurant bills, but not a service charge. A tip of 5 to 10 per cent will suffice.

Some of the best restaurants are to be found away from the towns, but bear in mind that the quality of the food in that charming farmhouse will not necessarily live up to the setting. When choosing a restaurant, look for somewhere where the majority of customers are locals. Steer clear of chains and places with picture menus or national flags. Eating out in Ibiza is an informal and relaxed affair and dress codes are rare.

Vegetarians

While Spain in general has been slow in catering for vegetarians, Ibiza is somewhat ahead of the game in this respect, although restaurants catering specifically for vegetarians and vegans are still thin on the ground. That said, in international restaurants at least, there should be at least one vegetarian main course on the menu, while gourmet establishments will, if forewarned, prepare vegetarian or even vegan meals. The humble country inn or farmhouse, however, may not be able to provide anything more exciting than soup, tomato salad or the dreaded omelette. It's best to double-check vegetarian-sounding dishes, as they are sometimes flavoured with ham or cod, or with animal stock.

Typical meals and ingredients

Starters

Arròs sec – thick soup with rice, fish, shellfish and prawns, lightly fried chicken, rabbit and vegetables.
Cassoleta de patates – casserole made with potatoes, onion, tomato, garlic and parsley.
Olla fresca – casserole made with haricot beans, broad beans, potatoes and pears.
Pa torrat amb tomata – toasted bread, rubbed with tomato, with a dribble of olive oil and a sprinkling of salt (also eaten at breakfast).
Sopa de menuts – chicken giblet soup.
Sopa de pa – bread soup, enriched with beaten egg.
Truita pagesa – potato omelette made with peppers and tomatoes.

Meat dishes

Caragols – snails, cooked with meats and pork fat.
Conill amb pebrots vermells – rabbit with red peppers.
Costelletes de moltó – rib of lamb, particularly tasty when served with *prebassos*, a local wild mushroom.
Llom de porc – charcoal grilled loin of pork, seasoned with rosemary.
Perdiu amb col – partridge served with cabbage and potatoes.
Sobrassada i botifarrons – spicy sausage meat, served with pork fat, potatoes and chicken broth.
Sofrit pagès – rich, hold-all hotpot, including Balearic sausage, pork, potatoes, onions, tomatoes, fried peppers and herbs.

Fish dishes

Amanida de peix – fish salad, a speciality of Formentera.

Bullit de peix – fish stew with potatoes, vegetables and chick peas.
Burrida de ratjada – stew made with potatoes and ray fish, cooked in a wine and spice stock with pulverised almonds and sometimes a few drops of pastis liqueur added.
Caldereta de langusta – lobster stew, originating in Menorca, cooked in a wooden casserole dish with onion, tomato, garlic and parsley.
Guisat de peix – fish stew made with grouper, bream, angler, scorpion fish or any other fresh fish available, plus garlic, onion, saffron, parsley, potatoes and cinnamon.
Tonyina a l'eivissenca – tuna seasoned with white wine, raisins, eggs, pine kernels, spices and lemon.

Desserts

Bunyols – small potato doughnuts, sprinkled with sugar.
Flaó – tart made with eggs, cheese, flour, sugar, aniseed and mint. Traditionally eaten at Easter.
Greixonera – the local version of crème caramel, made with egg yolks, milk and sugar, broken biscuits, with cinnamon and a slice of lemon. Sometimes with a few drops of *frígola* liqueur added.
Orelletes – popular cakes made with sugar and dried fruits.

Drinks

Frígola – Ibizan liqueur extracted from thyme, with an anise base.
Hierbas Ibicencas – popular liqueur flavoured with many herbs, including aniseed, thyme and rosemary, served chilled with a twist of lemon and orange peel.
Palo – Ibizan aperitif to be taken with a few drops of gin.
Vi de taula pagès – table wine. The quality of Ibizan table wines (whites and reds) has improved noticeably in recent years (*see pp170–71*). However, the same cannot be said for the rougher Formenteran varieties.

Spanish tapas

Aceitunas – green or black olives, sometimes stuffed with pepper or baby gherkins.
Anchoas – anchovies, usually served in vinegar. (Also known as *boquerrones.*)
Berberechos – cockles.
Chorizo – spicy sausage, served in the same way as *jamón serrano.*
Croquetas – made with thick béchamel sauce, chicken or chopped ham, and then deep-fried.
Ensaladilla rusa – Russian salad, with potatoes, vegetables and mayonnaise.
Gambas – shrimps grilled in their shells (*a la plancha*) or peeled and then fried in oil and garlic (*al ajillo*).
Jamón serrano – cured ham, served on its own, in slices.
Morcilla – very rich black pudding.
Patatas alioli – boiled potatoes with garlic and mayonnaise dressing.
Pimientos rellenos – peppers stuffed with meat, tuna or cod.
Pulpo – octopus.
Queso manchego – cheese made with sheep's milk, often coated with olive oil.

Restaurants

Meal prices

Meals at Ibizan restaurants can vary widely in price. The following price ranges should only be used as a rough guide. They are based on a meal for two including wine and tax.

★	Under €60
★★	€60–80
★★★	€80–100
★★★★	Over €100

EIVISSA

Cafe Sidney ★–★★

A relaxing café on the marina that is great for breakfast, lunch or just a coffee. There's Internet access and digital TV for entertainment, and it serves international cuisine.

Marina Botafoc.
Tel: 971 19 22 43; www.cafesidney.es

El Bistro ★★★

Subtly prepared French Mediterranean cooking is the hallmark of this restaurant on the lower road to Dalt Vila. The menu changes regularly, but if they have the duck magret in fig sauce, look no further. Should you be unable to find a table in the dining room, there is a terrace.

Sa Carrossa 15.
Tel: 971 39 32 03.
Open: Easter–Oct.

Can'Alfredo ★★★

One of Eivissa's best-known restaurants in a 19th-century mansion. Offers a large selection of typical Ibizan dishes, including delicious *arroz con sepia* (cuttlefish served with rice). Meticulous service and attention to detail.

Passeig de Vara de Rey 16.
Tel: 971 31 12 74. Closed: Mon & Nov.

Can den Parra ★★★

Dine by candlelight on the steps of a vine-covered terrace in Dalt Vila. Flavoursome, Spanish Mediterranean cooking – try the sautéed spinach with goats' cheese to start with, then the grilled sea bass made to an old Spanish recipe. Booking recommended throughout August.

Carrer Sant Rafel 3.
Tel: 971 39 11 14/ 30 39 01. Open: May–Oct, evenings only.

El Cigarral ★★★

This restaurant in a pretty house in the port area has a reputation for sophisticated Mediterranean cooking and specialises in game. Castilian-Spanish influences are at work in the more creative dishes.

Fray Vicente Nicolás 9.
Tel: 971 31 12 46.
Open: daily except Sun evening.

El Olivo ★★★

This classy French restaurant in Dalt Vila is renowned throughout the island for its refined Provençal cuisine, extensive wine list, refined ambience and attentive service. Booking essential.

Plaça de la Vila 7-g.
Tel: 971 30 06 80; www.elolivoibiza.org.
Open: evenings only.

Studio ★★★

Arabic décor and a French-inspired menu are on offer in this chic eatery. Eat on the balcony, on the terrace or inside.

Carrer de la Verge 4.
Tel: 971 31 53 68. Open: evenings only.

La Brasa ★★★★

Always in vogue thanks to its lovely, flower-filled, Arabic garden in summer

and log fire in winter. The extensive menu of grilled meat and fish dishes varies according to the season. Booking recommended.
Carrer Pere Sala 3.
Tel: 971 30 12 02.
Closed: Sun & Feb.

Figueretes

Soleado ★★★
There are at least two good reasons for recommending this French restaurant. One is the views of Formentera from the terrace, the other, wonderfully delicate Provençal cooking expertly prepared by the Avignon-trained chef.
Passeig Marítim Ses Figueretes.
Tel: 971 39 48 11.
Open: May–Oct.

Jesús: Sant Rafel de sa Creu

El Ayoun ★★★
For an echo of Ibiza's Arab past, try this superb Moroccan restaurant just north of the village. Both the interior décor and Bedouin tented garden are Moorish-inspired. Expensive but worth it.
Carrer Isidor Macabich 6.
Tel: 971 19 83 35;
www.elayoun.com.
Open: daily Easter–Oct.

L'Elephant ★★★
An elegant dining room and rooftop bar with wonderful views of Eivissa's historic centre. Superb French cuisine, exquisitely presented.
In front of the old white church.
Tel: 971 19 80 56;
www.elephant-ibiza.com

SANTA EULÀRIA AND THE EAST

Cala Boix

La Noria ★★
There are lovely sea views from this unassuming restaurant overlooking the beach, where the house speciality is the Balearic lobster stew, *caldereta de langosta.*
Cala Boix, Pou d'es Lleó.
Tel: 971 63 88 06/ 33 53 97.

Cala Llonga

La Casita ★★
Farmhouse restaurant in a beautiful setting overlooking a valley of pine trees. It specialises in Austrian and creative cuisine served in intimate candlelit dining rooms or on the terrace.
Urbanització Valverde, near Cala Llonga.
Tel: 971 33 02 93.
Closed: Tue & Sun.

Santa Eulària des Riu

Cardamom Club ★★
An old farmhouse is home to this excellent Indian restaurant where diners can eat under trailing grapevines in summer, and by a real open fire in winter. DJ Friday evenings and cocktails served on the terrace.
Sequia des Mallorquins, Can Flux, Puig de Misa.
Tel: 971 33 00 17.
Closed: Tue.

La Paella ★★
A cosmopolitan menu is served on the shady terrace of this restaurant. As well as paella, you can also order spaghetti, goulash or schnitzels. Children's menu available.
Urbanització Siesta 36.
Tel: 971 33 09 02.

Restaurante La Rambla ★★
A cosy restaurant right in the centre of town, with a lovely, leafy garden. European and

Spanish cuisine, with seafood and duck as specialities.
Passeig de S'Alamera 18. Tel: 971 33 08 57. Closed: Mon.

Bambuddha Grove ★★★
Bambuddha Grove serves an eclectic mix of fusion dishes, best described as Asian-Mediterranean. Guests dine by candlelight beneath a pyramid roof made from reeds and bamboo. Deli open for lunch daily.
Ctra de Sant Joan 8.5km. Tel: 971 19 75 10; www.bambuddha.com. Open: Apr–May Tue–Sun, June–Oct daily; open evenings only.

Ca Na Ribes ★★★
Restaurant with a distinguished pedigree for Ibizan and Mediterranean fish and meat dishes. Lovely indoor patio.
Carrer de Sant Jaume 67. Tel: 971 33 00 06. Open: Apr–Oct daily except Tue.

Celler C'an Pere ★★★
Wine casks and wood-beamed ceilings are the main decorative features of this large restaurant with charming courtyard. The fresh fish is cooked to perfection.
Carrer de Sant Jaume 63. Tel: 971 33 00 56. Open: daily evenings only.

The Royalty ★★★
One of the oldest café-restaurants on the island, The Royalty was a Fascist haunt during the Civil War, according to American writer Elliot Paul. The café serves up good breakfasts and desserts, while at the back you'll find an exclusive restaurant with an international menu.
Carre de Sant Jaume 51. Tel: 971 33 13 92.

SERRA DE ELS AMUNTS

Cala Sant Vicent

Can Gat ★★
Authentic Ibizan seafood and meat restaurant with terrace overlooking the beach. *Caldereta de langosta* to die for.
Sant Joan de Labritja. Tel: 971 32 01 23. Open: Apr–Nov.

SANT ANTONI DE PORTMANY

Cala Gracioneta

El Chiringuito ★★★
Not just any *chiringuito* (beach shack). Here the fish and paella are served almost at the water's edge, and the lighting is provided by candles floating on the water.
Tel: 971 34 83 38. Open: May–Oct.

Cala Salada

Cala Salada ★
Ibizan cooking at its no-frills best, right on the doorstep of one of the island's most arresting beaches. The fish comes straight from the owners' boat.
Platja de Cala Salada. Tel: 971 34 28 67.

Sant Antoni (Bay)

Es Pi d'Or ★★
Located at the northern end of the Bahía de Sant Antoni, this restaurant serves fish and seafood dishes based on Galician (northwestern Spanish) recipes. The judiciously chosen wine list is an additional recommendation.
Urbanització Cap Negret. Cala Gració. Tel: 971 34 28 72. Open: Tue–Sun. Closed: Mon & Dec–Feb.

Villa Mercedes ★★
In an old villa and garden in a spectacular location overlooking the

bay. Have a drink first in the bar or in the Karma Bar before enjoying the Mediterranean, Moorish-influenced food.
Passeig del Mar.
Tel: 971 34 85 43.

Banyan Palace Thai Restaurant ★★★
Stylish restaurant and gardens, where Thai food is served with local flavours, such as Ibizan liqueurs.
Outskirts of Sant Antoni Bay, on road to Port des Torrent.
Tel: 971 34 77 35; www.banyan-palace.com.
Open: Tue–Sun.

Can Pujol ★★★★
Small beach restaurant with a seaside terrace, tucked between the bars and hotels of Port des Torrent. The pick of the fish and seafood dishes is the house speciality, *bullit de peix.*
Port des Torrent. Tel: 971 34 14 07. Open: daily except Wed & Dec.

Sa Capella ★★★★
This restaurant on the road towards Santa Agnès has acquired a certain cachet thanks to the rich and famous among its clientele. The jury is out on the quality of the food, but no one will argue that the location, an abandoned 18th-century church and garden, is anything but evocative.
Camí de Cas Ramons, off Ctra Sant Antoni-Santa Agnès. Tel: 971 34 00 57.
Open: Apr–Oct evenings.

Sant Antoni (Town)

Curry Club ★★
A real oasis in Sant Antoni. Enjoy authentic Indian and Eastern cuisine in the tropical garden or in the exotically decorated restaurant.
Carrer Sant Antoni 38.
Tel: 971 34 36 04.
Open: Apr–Oct.

Tijuana Tex-Mex ★★
With its bold Mexican décor, this is the perfect place for authentic Tex-Mex salads, nachos, quesadillas, tortillas, pork ribs and even vegetarian fajitas.
Ramón i Cajal 23.
Tel: 971 34 24 73; www.tijuanatexmex.com

SANT JOSEP AND THE SOUTH

Cala d'Hort

Es Boldado ★★
Friendly *chiringuito* restaurant only a 5-minute walk from the beach. The seafood menu includes lobster and a small choice of typical Ibizan dishes, but the big draw is the view of Es Vedrà. Booking advisable.
Carrer des Torrent 25.
No phone; www.restauranteboldado.com

Cala Jondal

Tropicana ★★★
Thatched roof, flower-bedded patio and sea views distinguish this bar-restaurant on the right of the beach as you leave the car park. The fish casseroles are good.
Cala Jondal.
Tel: 971 80 26 40; www.tropicanaibiza.com.
Open: May–Sept.

Cala Tarida

Rincón de Tarida ★★
Traditional cuisine with a good choice of specials and an all-you-can-eat buffet on Sundays and Thursdays.
Plaça del Mar.
Tel: 971 80 64 45.
Open: daily in summer.

Cala Vedella

Maria Luisa ★★

Family-run establishment at the far end of the beach, serving typical fish, meat and seafood dishes, including mouthwatering crab. Booking advised, especially at weekends.
Cala Vedella.
Tel: 971 80 80 12.
Open: Tue–Sun.

Sant Agustí des Vedrà

Can Berri Vell ★★

Wonderfully atmospheric farmhouse in a village deep in the countryside. Be sure to book and try to arrive before sunset.
Plaça Major.
Tel: 971 34 43 21.
Open: Apr–end Oct daily, evenings only (closed Sun Apr, May & Oct).

Sant Josep

El Destino ★

Friendly bar-restaurant in the centre of the village that has a great line in Spanish tapas, with a hint of Pacific Rim flavours. There's plenty of choice, and vegetarians will not be disappointed. Couscous and tagine dishes on Moroccan nights (Friday).
Carrer Atalaya 15.
Tel: 971 80 03 41.
Open: daily except Sun.

FORMENTERA

Caló de Sant Agustí

Rafalet ★

This large waterfront restaurant prides itself on its Balearic fish and seafood dishes. The *bullit de peix* should not be overlooked. Reservations essential.
Venda Es Carnatge.
Tel: 971 32 70 77.
Open: May–Sept.

El Pilar de La Mola

La Pequeña Isla ★★

This unassuming roadside restaurant (with terrace) serves up simple island fare: roast rabbit, lamb and rice-based dishes.
Avda El Pilar 101.
Tel: 971 32 70 68.

El Mirador ★★

Located fairly discreetly at the right-hand side of the road, so the breathtaking views of Formentera come as something of a surprise. The menu includes paella, grilled fish and a selection of rice dishes. Booking essential in July and August.
Ctra El Pilar, 14km.
Tel: 971 32 70 37.
Open: May–Oct.

Es Pujols

Caminito ★★★

This well-established Argentinian steakhouse is the real McCoy, with a melt-in-the-mouth *asado de tira bife* and delicious sauces.
Ctra Es Pujols–La Savina.
Tel: 971 32 81 06.
Open: Apr–Nov, evenings only.

Sant Ferran

Real Playa ★★★

Restaurant on the beach serving Mediterranean cuisine and specialising in *fidegua au* fish from the island.
Platja Mitjorn.
Tel: 971 187 61.
Open: Apr–Oct.

La Savina

Aigüa ★★★★

Spanish restaurant with a touch of class and a terrace looking out onto the marina.
La Savina harbour.
Tel: 971 32 33 22; www.aiguaformentera.com.
Open: May–Sept.

Ibizan wines

A small bodega near Sant Josep caused a minor sensation when one of its wines was chosen for special mention at a tasting organised by an influential trade magazine. Praise indeed for a region that was not even on the viniculture map until the 1990s. The wine in question, Es Diví sa selecció 2001, was produced by Vins de Tanys Mediterranis, one of four bodegas on the island.

Modest beginnings

Wine was first brought to Ibiza by the Phoenicians in the 7th or 6th century BC – amphorae from the Pitiusas have been found in a number of ports around the Mediterranean, especially off the Valencian coast of Spain. Techniques improved during the Roman occupation when, it is said, orgiastic rites were celebrated with the encouragement of Bacchus himself. Following the expulsion of the

Tending a vine in a San Mateu vineyard

Moors in the 13th century, Jaume I was quick to grant new licences to aspiring winegrowers, but there were few takers in Ibiza. When Archduke Ludwig Salvator of Austria visited the island in 1867, he reported seeing only a tiny amount of land under cultivation, and this was before the phylloxera blight arrived from France. The wine that did eventually reach the table was coarse, and all of it was consumed before the following harvest. It was not until the 1980s that a handful of enterprising producers decided to invest in modern technology in a move to improve the quality of local wine. The gambit paid off: in 1996 the Balearic government was sufficiently impressed to designate Ibiza and Formentera a region with wines of a distinctive character – *Vinos de la Tierra* – and in 2003 it added regulatory controls. The aim now is to go one better and gain Ibizan Regional Wines the coveted *Denominación de Origen* (DO) status.

A growing business

The land under cultivation, currently around 130ha (321 acres), yields a modest 420 hectolitres (9,240 gallons) per annum, but there are plans to expand. Fifty per cent of the wine comes from the San Mateu valley and most of that from Joan Bonet's bodega at Sa Cova. There are three other wineries on the island: Vins de Tanys Mediterranis (*see opposite*), Can Maymó and Can Rich de Buscastell are near Sant Antoni. Conditions for growing wine are good – the reddish soil is rich in limestone and the climate typically Mediterranean with plenty of sunshine, mild winters and a modest amount of rainfall.

Traditionally, producers favoured the red Monastrell and Garnacha grapes and the Malabeo for the whites, but the new vineyards are experimenting with Cabernet Sauvignon, Merlot and Syrah (red) and Chardonnay, Muscatel or Viognier (white). One of the more unusual characteristics of Ibizan wine is the hint of aromatic herbs – thyme is used to prevent the blocking of the vats during fermentation. To date, varieties are almost exclusively *vinos de crianza* (table wines), but the quality is improving all the time. Who knows, Ibizan wines may, at the very least, be able to give the vineyards of Mallorca a run for their money.

Where to taste

The yield from the new harvest is showcased in December at the San Mateu wine festival. Otherwise, informal tours can be arranged in advance with either **Sa Cova** (*tel: 971 18 70 46. www.sacovaibiza.com*) or **Can Rich** (*tel: 971 80 33 77. www.bodegascanrich.com*). Local wines are on sale at **ENOTECUM** (*Avenida Isidor Macabich 34, Eivissa. www.enotecum-vins.com*) and at restaurants specialising in Ibizan cuisine.

Accommodation

Between them, Ibiza and Formentera receive nearly two million visitors every year, and the number of hotel beds is continually increasing to meet the demand. Bear in mind, however, that package tour companies block-book much of the medium-priced accommodation during July and August, making finding a room of any kind difficult.

There are six five-star hotels on Ibiza, with one more in the pipeline. Visitors can choose from the full range of accommodation, from luxury hotels with every conceivable amenity to the humble pension or hostel. Apartments outnumber hotels on Formentera, and at the height of the season demand outstrips supply. Prices are somewhat higher than on the mainland, but outside the peak season most establishments offer big reductions, so it is worth shopping around.

The tourist office produces a booklet, *Rural Tourism*, listing hotels offering alternative holidays in idyllic, natural surroundings far from the madding crowd. They are mostly converted farmhouses in extensive grounds. Facilities tend to be luxurious and are priced accordingly. Horse riding and other country pursuits (special hiking tours, for example) are often available. These are listed at the end of this section under 'Rural Hotels' (*pp178–9*).

Below is a selection of hotels and other accommodation on both Ibiza and Formentera. Unless otherwise indicated, they can be assumed to have en-suite facilities, telephone and TV. Most hotels accept payment by credit card, but some of the cheaper pensions will insist on cash.

Booking

Booking ahead is always advisable and an absolute must if you plan to visit during *Semana Santa* (Holy Week), during the local *ferias* (*see list on pp22–3*) or in the high season (roughly from the middle of July to the end of August). Hotels will normally hold rooms until 6pm, or later if you warn them of your estimated arrival time, but some may require pre-booking by credit card. Be warned that many do not quote prices inclusive of 17 per cent IVA, Spain's value-added tax. Checkout is usually at noon, but most hotels will keep bags or even let you use the room until later, if asked.

Prices

The prices shown according to the star system are average summertime prices for a double room. Suites and rooms during premium periods will be extra.

★ under €60
★★ €60–120
★★★ €120–180
★★★★ €180–300

EIVISSA

Hostal Mar Blau ★★
Wonderful sea views from this small, family hotel on Puig des Molins, only a short walk from the centre of town. Rooms, though strictly no-frills, are attractive enough and each has its own balcony or terrace. Bar and rooftop terrace.
Carrer Els Molins, Puig des Molins. Tel: 971 30 12 84. Open: May–Oct.

Hostal la Marina ★★
An old favourite on the seafront offers a variety of brightly painted rooms, some with balcony and jacuzzi. Discounts are available for longer bookings.
Carrer Barcelona 7.
Tel: 971 31 01 72;
www.hostal-lamarina.com

Hostal Parque ★★
Definitely the best budget option in town, this medium-sized *hostal* (29 rooms) is only a stone's throw from the walls of Dalt Vila. Though on the small side, rooms are pristine, with air conditioning and TV. Not all have baths. There is a rooftop sun terrace and a downstairs café. Popular, so advance booking is essential.
Plaça del Parc 4.
Tel: 971 30 13 58;
www.hostalparque.com

Can Pere ★★★
Golfing enthusiasts will love this sensitively converted 19th-century farmhouse nestling in delightful countryside only a short drive from the capital. Facilities include a swimming pool and a small restaurant.
On the Cala Llonga road, 1km (2/3 mile) west of Roca Llisa golf course.
Tel: 971 19 66 00;
www.canpereibiza.com

El Corsario ★★★
This one-time pirates' den in the heart of Dalt Vila was the home of a famous 19th-century corsair. The 14 smallish rooms have beamed roofs and antique furnishings (ask for one with a harbour view). Attractive rates out of season.
Carrer Poniente 5.
Tel: 971 30 12 48;
www.elcorsario-ibiza.com

El Hotel ★★★★
This new, minimalist, whiter-than-white hotel is owned by Pacha and is just minutes away from the club of the same name. All rooms are suites and the bar and restaurant are as stylish and lively as you would expect from this highly regarded stable.
Passeig Marítim.
Tel: 971 31 59 63;
www.elhotelpacha.com

Royal Plaza ★★★★
Modern hotel with comfortable rooms and all mod cons. The main recommendation, though, apart from the Le Relais restaurant, has to be the roof-top swimming pool with its wonderful views of the port and the Old Town.
Carrer Pere Francés 27–9.
Tel: 971 31 00 00;
www.hotelroyalplaza.net

La Torre del Canónigo ★★★★
You can't beat the location of this apart-hotel – next door to the cathedral in Dalt Vila – and the 14th-century defence tower is a listed building. All rooms have Old Town or harbour views, plus there's a sauna and steam room.
Carrer Major 8, Dalt Vila. Tel: 971 30 38 84; www.latorredelcanonigo.com. Open: Easter–New Year.

Figueretes

Es Vivé ★★★
A trendy hotel, popular with visiting DJs working the bars and clubs near Figueretes and Platja d'en Bossa beaches. Rooms are airy and pleasant, if on the small side. Some have sea views.
Carrer Carles Roman Ferrer 8. Tel: 971 30 19 02; www.ibiza-spotlight.com/esvive

Platja d'en Bossa

Hotel Club Goleta ★★★★
Large resort hotel, part of the Sirenis chain. A great place to relax, especially out of season, when it is surprisingly quiet and prices drop substantially. The beach is close to hand, the rooms are comfortable and the amenities outstanding – spa, sauna, jacuzzi, swimming pool, table tennis and billiards.
Avda Pere Matutes Noguera. Tel: 971 30 21 58; www.sirenishotels.com

Jesús: Platja de Talamanca

Argos ★★
Sea views are the main draw of this recently refurbished, medium-size hotel on a beach between Eivissa and Talamanca bays. All rooms are of a generous size, and there are two pools, one for children.
Tel: 971 31 21 62.

Hostal Talamanca ★★
Modern low-rise building in a quiet location directly overlooking the beach but with shops, bars, restaurants and public transport close to hand.
Tel: 971 31 24 63; www.hostaltalamanca-ibiza.com

Hotel Lux Isla ★★
Small hotel only a short walk from the beach but within easy reach of Eivissa. All rooms have satellite TV and most have balconies with sea views.
Carrer Josep Pla 1. Tel: 971 31 34 69; www.luxisla.com

Victoria Hotel ★★
The beachside location of this competitively priced hotel makes it a favourite with families. Most of the rooms have sea views.
Platja de Talamanca. Tel: 971 31 19 12; www.victoriahotel-ibiza.com

SANTA EULÀRIA AND THE EAST

Sant Carles de Peralta

Can Curreu ★★★★
This farmhouse enjoys a peaceful wooded setting in the hills west of Las Dalias. The restaurant is excellent and facilities include a jacuzzi, swimming pool, gym and solarium.
Ctra Sant Carles, km 12. Tel: 971 33 52 80; www.cancurreu.com

Es Canar

Las Arenas ★★
A good-value, warm and

cosy family-run *hostal* on the beach, facing the fishing port of Es Canar. The hotel also has a rooftop terrace with the same sea views. It is well located for taking walks around the countryside inland.
Tel: 971 33 07 90; www.lasarenasibiza.com

Es Figueral

Invisa Hotel Club Cala Blanca ★★
This large hotel offers excellent value for money and caters for families, with a children's pool, club and playground. It has first-rate sporting facilities, including tennis, archery and water polo.
Platja d'Es Figueral.
Tel: 971 33 51 00; www.invisa-hoteles.com

Santa Eulària des Riu

Ca's Català ★★
Friendly, English-run hotel at the foot of Puig d'en Missa, close to the restaurants, shops and beaches of the new town. Comfortable en-suite rooms and shady courtyard with small pool and sun terrace. No children.
Carrer del Sol.
Tel: 971 33 10 06; www.cascatala.com

Palladium ★★★★
Located near the river in Santa Eulària's beach 'suburb', this luxury hotel occupies a historic building inspired by classic Palladian architecture. Health and relaxation treatments, including thalassotherapy, are a speciality.
Carrer els Lliris 1, Siesta.
Tel: 971 33 82 60; www.aaapalladium.com

Rio Mar ★★★
This hotel is on the river side of town but within comfortable walking distance of the centre. All 120 simply furnished rooms have en-suite bathrooms and a terrace with either sea or mountain views.
Platja els Pins.
Tel: 971 33 03 27; www.hotelriomar.com.
Open: May–Sept.

S'Argamassa Palace ★★★★
Modern, recently refurbished hotel in attractive grounds, handily situated for exploring. There is a decent-sized pool, a restaurant and children's playground and garden area.
Urbanització S'Argamassa.
Tel: 971 33 02 71; www.sargamassa-palace.com

Tres Torres ★★★
Convenience and comfort are the twin advantages of this modern hotel overlooking the marina and only a few minutes' walk to the beach. Sea views from all rooms.
Badia Ses Estaques.
Tel: 971 33 03 26.

Can Parramatta ★★★★
Intimate villa built at the beginning of the 20th century, surrounded by olive groves. There is a large pool and an attractive terraced area.
Sa Rota den Cosmi 63.
Tel: 971 33 69 43; www.parramatta-ibiza.com

SERRA DE ELS AMUNTS

Portinatx

La Ciguenya ★★
A beach hotel with a loyal clientele, it has its own restaurant with views of the bay from the terrace, swimming pool (heated in May and October) and gym.

It also offers car hire and has bicycles available free of charge for the use of guests.
S'Arenal Petit 36, Cala Portinatx. Tel: 971 32 06 14; www.laciguenya.com

Hostal Cas Mallorquí ★★–★★★
Nine modern, comfortable rooms with sea views, TV, private bathrooms and air conditioning in a beautiful setting near one of Ibiza's most prized coves. Excellent value.
Cala Portinatx. Tel: 971 32 05 05; www.casmallorqui.com.

El Greco ★★–★★★
Large hotel in a quiet, pine-wooded location overlooking S'Arenal beach, with panoramic sea views and a water-park for children.
Cala Portinatx. Tel: 971 32 05 70; www.ibiza-spotlight.com/elgreco

Presidente ★★★
Situated in pine woods, this large tourist hotel with all mod cons is just a short hop from the beach.
Cala Portinatx. Tel: 971 32 05 76; www.hotelpresidenteibiza.com

Sant Miquel de Balansat

Hotel Hacienda Na Xamena ★★★★
The first and, for a long time, the only five-star hotel on the island is a real classic. The 74 exquisite rooms sit on a cliff top in a blissful setting of pools and terraces. A real gem.
Urbanització Na Xamena. Tel: 971 33 45 00; www.hotelhacienda-ibiza.com

Santa Agnès de Corona

Can Pujolet ★★★★
This early 20th-century farmhouse, converted to suit 21st-century tastes, is situated in the hills to the northeast of the village and is the perfect location for mountain biking and horse riding. Breakfast is included and all rooms feature a terrace.
2.5km (1½ miles) northeast of Santa Agnès. Tel: 971 80 51 70; www.ibizarural.com

Es Cucons ★★★★
This beautiful, stylish 17th-century converted farmhouse enjoys a superb rural setting in the peaceful seclusion of the Ibizan countryside. Highly recommended.
2km (1¼ miles) southwest of Santa Agnès. Tel: 971 80 55 01; www.escucons.com

Sant Joan de Labritja

Casa Vilda Marge ★★★
This renovated, 400-year-old farm lies in beautiful countryside, and traditional livestock farming still continues here. The five rooms share four bathrooms in this lovely, rustic setting.
Venda de Xarraca 10, Ctra. Portinatx. Tel: 971 33 32 34; www.casavildamarge.com

Can Marti ★★★–★★★★
This family-run organic farm lies in a beautiful valley overlooked by hills planted with olives, almonds and carob trees. Home-produced fruit and vegetables are available, likewise organic breakfasts. Magnificent beaches are

just a short drive away.
1km ($^2/_3$ mile) west of Sant Joan.
Tel: 971 33 35 00; www.canmarti.com.
Open: Mar–Oct.

Atzaró ★★★★
This achingly cool *finca* comes complete with spa, restaurant and cocktail lounge. All rooms have a terrace.
Ctra San Juan, km 15.
Tel: 971 33 88 38; www.atzaro.com

SANT ANTONI DE PORTMANY

Bahía de Sant Antoni

Hostal Residencia Salada ★
The rooms in this small, centrally located hotel are spotless and a good size. Only some have balconies and en-suite bathrooms, though, so book well ahead.
Carrer Soletat 24.
Tel: 971 34 11 30.
Open: Easter–Oct.

Osiris Ibiza ★–★★
All 97 rooms in this family-run hotel overlooking the beach at Es Puet have sea or garden views. Buffet-restaurant and swimming pool. Excellent value.
Platja Es Puet.
Tel: 971 34 09 16; www.hotelosiris.com

Hotel-Club Els Pins ★★
Large, modern hotel with simply furnished rooms and a pool, set in pine-wooded parkland between Cala Pinyet and S'Estanyol.
Carrer des Caló.
Tel: 971 34 03 01.

Fiesta Hotel Cala Gració ★★★
Ideally located in the peaceful cove of Cala Gració, but only a short hop from the town centre, this pretty *Ibizenco*-style hotel has lovely gardens leading down to the sea, and several areas in which to relax. It has 50 rooms.
Crta Cala Gració.
Tel: 971 34 13 00; www.fiestahotelgroup.com.

Vistabella ★★★
'Beautiful view' just about sums up this complex of 11 luxury bungalows in lovely grounds about 25 minutes' walk from town and with a stunning bay outlook. All rooms have tasteful furnishings and a terrace. Two pools (one for children) and riding school nearby.
Camí de Benamussi.
Tel: 971 34 23 24; www.vistabella.net

Pike's ★★★★
Deep in the countryside, yet less than five minutes' drive from the sea, this rambling 15th-century farmhouse has been transformed into a stylish hotel with 40 handsome bedrooms and suites. Excellent restaurant, floodlit swimming pool and tennis court, gym and sauna.
Camí de Sa Vorera.
Tel: 971 34 22 22; www.pikeshotel.com

SANT JOSEP AND THE SOUTH

Cala Molí

Hostal Cala Molí ★★
Family hostel in a wooded setting with easy access to some of the island's best beaches. The eight double rooms, tastefully decorated in rustic style, are built around a small pool overlooking the sea.
1km ($^2/_3$ mile) south of Cala Molí.
Tel: 971 80 60 02; www.calamoli.com

FORMENTERA

Cala Saona

Cala Saona ★★★★
The architecture of this standard, sugar-white modern block may not be very distinguished, but the location, behind this stunning pine-wooded bay, more than makes up for it. Large, airy rooms, each with balcony or terrace, and also tennis courts.
Sa Pujdada 1–9.
Tel: 971 32 20 30;
www.hotelcalasaona.com.
Open: Apr–Oct.

Caló de Sant Agustí

Hostal Residencia Mar Blau ★★
Excellent budget option near the fishing harbour and the beach at Ses Platgetes. Each of the ten rooms has a terrace with sea views. Bike and scooter hire available.
Sa Pujada 1–9.
Tel: 971 32 70 30.
Open: Apr–Oct.

Es Pujols

Hostal Roca Plana ★★
Good value, given the excellent location, overlooking the beach and only 1km (approx. 2/3 mile) from the Ses Salines National Park.
Carrer Espalmador 41–55.
Tel: 971 32 83 35;
www.rocaplana.es.
Open: May–Oct.

Hostal Voramar ★★–★★★
Friendly hotel with pool, close to the beach and the centre of Es Pujols. Rooms have air conditioning with bath or shower, and some are suitable for guests with disabilities.
Avda Miramar 25–31.
Tel: 971 32 81 19;
www.hostalvoramar.com

Roca Bella ★★★
The main charm of this hotel built in the 1950s is its location at the furthest end of the bay of Es Pujols. Bedrooms are simple, but some have terraces with sea views. It has no restaurant, but breakfast is served and there is a snack bar. Other facilities include a solarium and a swimming pool.
Platja Es Pujols.
Tel: 971 32 81 30.

La Savina

Micalet ★–★★
There is a pleasant family atmosphere at this basic but convenient guest house, located at a 5 minute walk from the Port and near the Estany des Peix.
Avenida Mediterranea 35.
Tel: 971 322 049.

Hostal La Savina ★★
The location of this popular *hostal* near the Estany des Peix (most rooms have lake views) is excellent for exploring the island.
Avda Mediterrania.
Tel: 971 32 22 79;
www.hotel-lasavina.com.
Open: May–Oct.

Hostal Bahía ★★★
Located in a modern building opposite the marina, the hotel's main asset is its bright, airy, tastefully furnished and spacious rooms, all with air conditioning, Wi-Fi access and TV. Not all have private balconies, but the hotel also has a large terrace.
Passeig de la Marina.
Tel: 971 32 21 42;
www.hbahia.com

Platja de Migjorn

Hotel Riu La Mola ★★★
Large, upmarket hotel at the La Mola end of Platja Migjorn. On-site

facilities include gym, tennis courts and mini-golf, with canoe and bike hire available.
Tel: 971 32 70 00; www.riu.com. Open: May–Oct.

Gecko Beach Club ★★★★
This tranquil *hostal* enjoys a pleasant pine-shaded setting just behind one of Formentera's most beautiful beaches. Some of the rooms have sea views, and the restaurant serves delicious, freshly caught fish. It has bicycles, motorcycles, cars and boat to rent.
Tel: 971 32 80 24; www.hrcostazul.com

Insotel Club Formentera Playa ★★★★
Large hotel (also self-catering studios) in a quiet beachfront location. Extensive gardens. Watersports such as scuba diving and sailing, and a kids' club.
Tel: 971 32 80 00; www.insotel.com

Platja de Sa Roqueta

Lago Playa ★★★
Small hotel also with bungalows and a pool near the beach at Sa Roqueta and within easy reach (1km/⅔ mile) of Es Pujols. It has a café and children's playground.
Tel: 971 32 85 07; www.lagoplaya.com. Open: mid-May–Oct.

Sant Ferran

Apartamentos Mayans ★★
Seven apartments, each with a private terrace in an attractive building near the centre of the village. Well situated for exploring the island, with Es Pujols and Platja Migjorn both close to hand.
Ctra Cala En Baster, km 3. Tel: 971 32 84 39.

OUTSIDE THE AREA

Palma Mallorca

Hotel Born ★★
Refurbished 16th-century mansion furnished in typical Mallorcan style, with a courtyard café and in a good central location. Book in advance.
Carrer Sant Jaume 3, Palma. Tel: 971 71 29 42; www.hotelborn.com

Convent de la Missió ★★★★
Acclaimed in the Spanish press, this hotel is in a restored 17th-century convent built for missionary priests. The striking modernist interiors, wine cellar and spa are all appealing. Book in advance.
Carrer de la Missió 7, Palma. Tel: 971 22 73 47; www.conventdelamissio.com

Mainland Spain

Hotel Costa Blanca ★★
Modern hotel with an ideal location only 50m (55yd) from the quayside, yet near the shopping and tourist areas.
Pintor Llorens 3, Dénia. Tel: (965) 78 03 36; www.hotelcostablanca.com

Hostal Venecia ★★
Excellent value, this hotel is handily situated for exploring the historic sights in the city. Highly recommended.
Plaza Ayuntamiento, Valencia. Tel: (963) 52 42 67; www.hotelvenecia.com

Practical guide

Arriving

Entry formalities

Visitors from the EU can enter Spain without a visa providing they have a valid national identity card or passport (valid for at least 3 months after the intended date of leaving the island). Citizens of Canada, New Zealand, the USA and Australia do not need a visa for stays of up to 90 days. It is advisable to consult with your tour company, airline or consulate before travelling.

Terrace views are a feature of many hotels on the islands

By air

Most visitors arrive by charter flights as part of a package holiday. **Thomas Cook** (*www.flythomascook.com*) fly to the island from London and some UK regional airports. **easyJet** (*tel: 0871 244 2366; www.easyjet.com*) offers flights from London Stansted, Gatwick and several regional airports.
British Airways (*tel: 0844 493 0787; www.ba.com*) flies from both Gatwick and Heathrow. **Flybe** operates from Southampton to Mallorca (*tel: 0871 700 2000; www.flybe.com*). **Iberia** (*tel: (902) 40 05 00; www.iberia.com*) and **Air Europa** (*tel: (902) 40 15 01; www.air-europa.com*) have scheduled flights to Ibiza via Madrid, Barcelona and other Spanish airports. Bear in mind that flights are heavily booked during the holiday season. The flight from the UK takes around 2½ hours.

Ibiza's international airport is at Sant Jordi, 7km (4 miles) southwest of Eivissa. Facilities include a tourist office (May–September only), ATMs and car rental (*tel: (902) 40 47 04*).

There is an bus service to Eivissa town centre every 20 minutes in summer, from 6.20am to midnight; and every 30 minutes in winter, from 7.20am to 23.50. The journey takes 30 minutes.

By ferry

There are regular services to Ibiza from the Spanish mainland and via Mallorca.

The main companies are:
Baleària *Tel: (902) 16 01 80;.* *www.balearia.com*
Trasmediterránea *Tel: (902) 45 46 45; www.trasmediterranea.es*

Details of ferry services can be found in the *Thomas Cook European Rail Timetable*, available to buy online at *www.thomascookpublishing.com*, from branches of Thomas Cook in the UK or *tel: (01733) 416477.*

Camping

There are only a handful of campsites in Ibiza and none at all in Formentera. All are open Easter to late October only. Camping outside official areas is illegal.
Camping Cala Bassa Near the beach, with all facilities. *Tel: 971 34 45 99; www.campingcalabassa.com*
Camping Cala Nova Near the beach. *Tel: 971 33 17 74; www.campingcalanova.com*

Children

Children up to age 12 travel half-price on public transport. Infants travel free. It is not advisable to bring babies younger than 2 to Ibiza during July and August because of the heat. Most hotels offer a babysitting service. Some hotels provide all-day care and special entertainment for youngsters. (*See pp156–7.*)

Consulates

Australia The nearest consulate is in Barcelona: *Plaça Gala Placida, 1–3, 1°. Tel: 93 490 9013. www.embaustralia.es*
Canada The nearest consulate is in Barcelona: *Plaça de Catalunya, 9-1°–2°. Tel: 93 412 72 36. www.canadainternational.gc.ca*
UK *Avda Isidoro Macabich 45, 1 Eivissa. Tel: 971 30 18 18.*
USA The nearest consulate is in Barcelona: *Passeig Reina Elisenda de Montcada 23. Tel: (093) 280 2227; www.embusa.es*

Crime and safety

Crime is not a major problem in Ibiza. There is little street violence, and women are generally able to walk around safely at night. Thefts do occur wherever there are crowds, so take

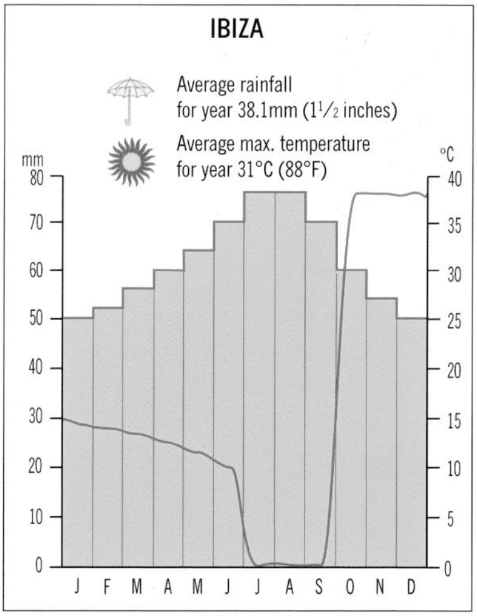

WEATHER CONVERSION CHART

25.4mm = 1 inch
°F = 1.8 × °C + 32

sensible precautions. Leave nothing valuable visible in a parked car, avoid carrying excessive amounts of cash and never leave valuables unattended. Where possible, leave valuables in an insured safety deposit box in your hotel or apartment. Report any loss to the police, who will give you a *denuncia* (written statement), which you need to keep for insurance claims. Lost or stolen passports should be reported to the appropriate consulate. It's a good idea to keep a separate list of passport details, traveller's cheque numbers, holiday insurance policy numbers and emergency phone numbers.

Customs regulations

The rules for duty-free allowances for people travelling between EU states (including between Spain and the United Kingdom) have been liberalised and broadly state that you may take with you reasonable amounts of tobacco products, alcohol and perfume, as long as they are for your personal consumption or use and not for resale. If you are thinking about buying and taking home large quantities of some item, you should first consult the customs authorities in your destination country. Non-EU residents may apply for VAT refunds on duty-free tourists' goods: to do this you will need a *formulari*, stamped by a customs officer as you leave. The refund can be claimed at the airport, by post or via a bank transfer.

Driving

To drive in Ibiza you need a full licence from any EU country, which you must carry with you at all times, together with your passport and all insurance and car-hire documentation. The Spanish drive on the right. Traffic on a roundabout has priority from the left. Speed limits are as follows: 120km/h (75mph) on motorways, 90km/h (56mph) on major roads and 50km/h (31mph) in towns. Children under 14 must travel in the back seat, and seat belts are compulsory at all times. The local police are vigilant and enforce drink-driving and other regulations, with random checks and hefty on-the-spot fines. Penalties for serious drink-driving offences have recently increased.

Outside the main towns, petrol pumps are uncommon, so make sure you fill up before setting off. Historic areas like Dalt Vila in Eivissa are closed to motor traffic, making for congestion elsewhere. Pavements marked with a blue line are designated pay-park areas. The system works on a 'pay and display' basis. Do not exceed the time indicated, as traffic wardens are 'clamp happy' and fines are prohibitive. Parking is usually free from 2–4pm and after 10pm, but check the schedules on the machines.

Hiring a car, motorcycle or scooter (a very popular option) opens up the possibility of exploring the furthest reaches of Ibiza in a relatively short space of time – no destination is further than 45km (28 miles). Cars are discouraged on Formentera for environmental reasons. To hire a car you must be over 21 and have held a full licence for at least two years. Check insurance cover for accident damage, vehicle theft and liability before you sign on the dotted line. The law requires that all cars carry a red warning triangle and replacement headlamp bulbs. Ask the rental company to confirm that these comply with regulations.

Avis, **Hertz** and **Europcar** have desks at the airport, but local firms offer cheaper rates.

Centauro Rent a Car: pick-up and return service at the airport, with a wide range of cars. *Tel: (902) 10 41 03; www.centauro.net*

Electricity

The voltage is 220V. Mains sockets take the standard European two-pin plugs.

Emergency telephone numbers

General emergencies (all services) *112*.
Red Cross emergency ambulance *(902) 22 22 92.*

Health

Avoid the beach between 1pm and 4pm. Always use a high-factor sunblock (don't forget to apply it to your feet) and make use of hired umbrellas. Reapply sunblock after going in the water – no sun cream is 100 per cent waterproof. Children should always wear T-shirts and hats. Local water is safe to drink, but bottled water tastes better. Doctors offer emergency care of the kind found in accident and emergency units in the UK, and basic medical advice and help can be provided by pharmacists (*farmacia*: look for the green cross, which is lit when the shop is open). Pharmacists display a list of which branch is open when, and in the resorts most pharmacists speak English.

Hospitals and Health Centres (*Centre de Salut*):
Eivissa, Hospital Can Misses, *Carrer de Corona. Tel: 971 39 70 10.*
Santa Eulària Health Centre, *Carrer Historiador Clapés. Tel: 971 33 24 53.*
Sant Antoni Health Centre, *Carrer Ses Sequies 6. Tel: 971 19 58 50.*
Santa Gertrudis Health Centre, *Vénda des Poble 20. Tel: 971 19 75 70.*
Formentera Health Centre, *Venda des Brolls. Tel: 971 32 12 12.*

Road train, Puig d'en Missa

Insurance

EU citizens are entitled to free emergency medical treatment – take with you an EHIC card (obtainable from post offices, by phoning *0845 606 0707* or online at *www.ehic.org.uk*). All visitors should also arrange insurance to cover non-urgent treatments and the costs of repatriation.

Maps

Make sure your map is marked in Catalan, as many signs are in Catalan, not Spanish.

Tourist information offices have town plans and maps of suggested hiking, cycling and driving routes. For hiking or cycling, the most detailed maps are produced by the Instituto Geográfico Nacional and are obtainable from specialist bookshops and at *www.ign.es*

Media

Many pubs and cafés have satellite TV (BBC, Sky, etc.), usually for sports fans.

Ibiza has no local English-language newspapers; however, international editions of British and German newspapers are available. *ibiza-online.com* is an online newsletter covering subjects such as tourism, politics and people (subscription only).

Money matters

The unit of currency is the euro. Notes range from 5–500 euros, coins from 1 céntimo to 2 euros. Euro coins and banknotes from other countries are all acceptable currency.

Multilingual ATMs are commonplace in the main towns but more of a rarity in the smaller seaside resorts and remoter villages. Most hotels, restaurants and shops accept credit cards, though pensions, *hostals*, smaller cafés and market stalls may insist on payment in cash. Bear in mind that if you are changing traveller's cheques, banks close at 2pm weekdays and 1pm Saturdays.

Opening hours

Museums and historic monuments are usually open Tue–Sun 10am–2pm and 4–6pm, but closed on public holidays and fiestas. Times are often reduced in the winter.

Offices work similar hours. Big department stores tend to open all day from 8 or 9am to 8pm, while many shops in the resorts remain open till late at night.

Banks are open Mon–Fri 9am–2pm, Sat 9am–1pm.

Ibiza's crystal-clear waters are a paradise for snorkellers

Language

An attempt to speak Catalan will win hearts, but if you have a little Spanish and want to practise it, very few people will mind. Try not to just bulldoze on in loud English!

English	**Catalan**	**Spanish**
yes	si	sí
no	no	no
please	sisplau	por favor
sorry	perdoni	perdón
thank you	gràcies	gracias
hello	hola	hola
goodbye	adéu	adiós
morning	matí	mañana
good day	bon dia	buenos días
good afternoon/evening	bona tarda	buenas tardes
good night	bona nit	buenas noches
do you speak English?	vostè parla Angles?	¿usted habla inglés?
I don't speak Catalan/Spanish	no parlo Català	yo no hablo Español
Where is…?	On està…?	¿Donde está…?
How much is…?	Quant val…?	¿Cuánto cuesta…?
breakfast	esmorzar	desayuno
lunch	dinar	almuerzo
dinner	sopar	cena
open	obert	abierto
closed	tancat	cerrado
help!	socors	socorro

Days of the week		
Monday	dilluns	lunes
Tuesday	dimarts	martes
Wednesday	dimecres	miércoles
Thursday	dijous	jueves
Friday	divendres	viernes
Saturday	dissabte	sábado
Sunday	diumenge	domingo

Police

There are three police forces in Ibiza: the Policía Nacional (state police) deal with serious incidents; the Policía Municipal (local police) patrol the small towns and resorts; and the Guardia Civil (National Guard) operate mostly in rural areas.
Policía Nacional *091*
Guardia Civil *062*
Emergencies *112*
Citizen's Advice *060*

Post offices

Postal services from the islands often take some time to reach their destination. If a message is urgent, use fax or email. The express (*urgente*) deliveries are not always as quick as they claim to be. Post offices are generally open Mon–Fri 9am–2pm and 5–7pm and Sat 9.30am–2pm. Stamps can also be bought from hotel desks and from tobacconists (*estanios*). Post boxes are yellow. The central post office is on *Avinguda Isidor Macabich 67, Eivissa.*

Public holidays

1 January *Any Nou* New Year's Day
6 January *Dia dels Reis* Epiphany
1 March *Dia de les Illes Balears* Balearic Self-Government Day
March/April (variable) *Divendres Sant* Good Friday
1 May *Dia dels Traballadors* Labour Day
May/June (variable) Corpus Christi
25 July *Sant Jaume* Feast of St James (Formentera only)
8 August *Sant Ciriac* (Eivissa only)
15 August *Assumpció de la Verge* Assumption of the Blessed Virgin Mary
12 October *Dia de la Hispanitat* National Day of Spain
1 November *Tot Sants* All Saints' Day
6 December *Dia de la Constitució* Constitution Day
8 December *Immaculada Concepció* Immaculate Conception
25 December *Nadal* Christmas Day

Public transport

Buses

The main bus station in Ibiza is in Eivissa (*Avda Isidor Macabich*). There is a café here if you have to wait for a bus. Tickets are sold in advance from the windows, where timetables and prices are posted. Few of the staff speak English, so it may be necessary to write down your destination. Bear in mind that most place names are still written in Castillian. This causes most confusion with Eivissa (Pueblo Ibiza). Buses link Eivissa to the main towns. The sign 'P' means *parada* (stop).

In Sant Antoni, the main bus terminus is opposite the ferry port. There are half-hourly services from here to Eivissa (Pueblo Ibiza on the timetable), via Sant Rafel and Sant Josef, and good connections to Port des Torrent and other nearby beaches.

A disco bus service (*Tel: 971 31 34 47*) operates hourly from midnight to dawn with routes linking all the clubs, but it gets very crowded in August. Autocares Paya operate a bus service that connects

La Savina with the main villages on Formentera. Information can be found at *www.ibizabus.com* and at *www.autocarespaya.com*

Ferries

Local ferries run (summer only) from Eivissa to Playa d'en Bossa and between Eivissa, Es Canar, Cala Llonga and Santa Eulària. In Sant Antoni there are shuttle services to Port des Torrent and other local beaches.

Boat services to Formentera (La Savina) depart from Sant Antoni and Santa Eulària in season, but the service is much less frequent than from Eivissa (departure Estación Maritima, Avda Santa Eulària), from where there are daily ferries in summer from 7am to 9.30pm. From Formentera to Ibiza there are ferries from 8.30am to 9pm. The journey takes around 30 minutes.

Taxis

Taxis are white with a diagonal stripe on both front doors. Taxis for hire always display a green light. Fares are charged on a meter system, based on mileage. Taxis to the airport charge an additional tariff.
Radio Taxi Eivissa *Tel: 971 39 84 83.*
Santa Eulària *Tel: 971 33 33 33.*
Sant Antoni *Tel: 971 34 37 64.*

Sustainable tourism

Thomas Cook is a strong advocate of ethical and fairly traded tourism and believes that the travel experience should be as good for the places visited as it is for the people who visit them. That's why we firmly support The Travel Foundation, a charity that develops solutions to help improve and protect holiday destinations, their environment, traditions and culture. To find out what you can do to make a positive difference to the places you travel to and the people who live there, please visit *www.makeholidaysgreener.org.uk*

Telephones

Public telephones, coin- or card-operated, can be found in kiosks and in bars and restaurants. Phonecards are sold in tobacconists. There are two types – one with a black magnetic strip, the other with a PIN.
Local calls are cheap. The most economical option for phoning abroad is the international phonecard. International calls are cheapest at night – between 10pm and 8am and on Sundays.

The code for Spain is *0034.*

The code for the Balearic Islands is *971* – dial all nine digits.

To call the UK, dial *0044* then the number, excluding the first zero.

Time

Ibiza, like the rest of Spain, is on Central European Time, one hour ahead of GMT (Greenwich Mean Time).

Tipping

Five to ten per cent is customary in bars and restaurants unless a service charge has already been taken.

Toilets

Public toilets are few and far between. Use the facilities in cafés, bars and restaurants whenever possible, but only if you are a customer.

Tourist Information

Spanish Tourist Board:

Canada: *2 Bloor Street West, 34th floor, Toronto M4W 3E2. Tel: (416) 961 3131. Email: toronto@tourspain.es*

UK: *7a New Cavendish St, London W1W 6XB (appointment only). Tel: (020) 7486 8077. Email: info.lourdes@tourspain.es*

USA: *666 Fifth Avenue, 35th floor, New York, NY 10103. Tel: (212) 265 8822. Email: newyork.information@tourspain.es.*

There is a tourist information desk at the airport on Ibiza. (*Open: all year. Tel: 971 80 91 18.*)

Tourist offices in the major resorts generally open 10am–2pm & 4–6pm. Smaller offices close during the winter.

Eivissa: *Vara del Rey 1. Tel: 971 30 19 00; www.ibiza.travel.es*

Sant Antoni: *Passeig de Ses Fonts. Tel: 971 34 33 63; www.santantoni.net*

Sunrise over Eivissa

An aerial view of Ibiza

Santa Eulària: *Mariano Riquer Wallis 4. Tel: 971 33 07 28; www.santaeularia.net*

Travellers with disabilities

Spain lags behind many European countries in this respect. Most hotels, museums and shops are difficult, if not impossible, for people with disabilities to access, as is public transport, although some buses are now being provided with ramps.

For further advice contact:

Federació ECOM (The Catalan Association for the Disabled)
Gran Via de les Corts Catalanes 562, principal 2a, Barcelona.
Tel: (934) 51 55 50; www.ecom.cat

COCEMFE (The Spanish Association for the Disabled)
Calle Luis Cabrera 63, Madrid.
Tel: (917) 44 36 00; www.cocemfe.es

Websites

www.ibiza-spotlight.com A guide for tourists, with an online booking service and lots of useful extras, such as maps and a clubbing calendar.
www.eivissa.es Office website of Eivissa's town hall, with a section dedicated to tourism in English.
www.ibiza-hotels.com Good, detailed information on beaches, as well as history, restaurant and hotel sections.
www.gayibiza.net All the information a gay visitor to the island could want.
www.digitalibiza.com Hosts forums and competitions and gives information about clubs and forthcoming events.

Index

Acknowledgements

Thomas Cook Publishing wishes to thank the following photographers, libraries and associations for the photographs reproduced in this book, to whom the copyright belongs.

ALAMY 1, 51, 57, 81
DREAMSTIME 15 (Forbfruit), 66 (Anne Giliam), 101 (Amanda Perkins), 103 (Cristian Nitu), 124, 159 (Lunamarina), 161 (Lola), 189 (Alexander Fahn-Womack)
JANE EGGINTON 7, 8, 49, 113
GETTY IMAGES 170
IBATUR 72, 98 (Manuela Muñoz), 109, 127 (Pedro Coll)
PICTURES COLOUR LIBRARY 79
SPANISH TOURIST OFFICE 23, 143, 145
JULIET STEVENSON 107
THOMAS COOK 24, 29, 64, 65, 85, 144, 147, 149
WIKIMEDIA COMMONS 130 (Samu), 135 (diluvi.com Anna i Adria)
WORLD PICTURES 17, 69, 97

The remaining pictures were taken by CAROLINE JONES.

For CAMBRIDGE PUBLISHING MANAGEMENT LIMITED:
Project editor: Thomas Willsher
Typesetter: Donna Pedley
Proofreaders: Lucilla Watson & Michele Greenbank

SEND YOUR THOUGHTS TO BOOKS@THOMASCOOK.COM

We're committed to providing the very best up-to-date information in our travel guides and constantly strive to make them as useful as they can be. You can help us to improve future editions by letting us have your feedback. If you've made a wonderful discovery on your travels that we don't already feature, if you'd like to inform us about recent changes to anything that we do include, or if you simply want to let us know your thoughts about this guidebook and how we can make it even better – we'd love to hear from you.

Send us ideas, discoveries and recommendations today and then look out for your valuable input in the next edition of this title.

Emails to the above address, or letters to the traveller guides Series Editor, Thomas Cook Publishing, PO Box 227, Coningsby Road, Peterborough PE3 8SB, UK.

Please don't forget to let us know which title your feedback refers to!